CUSTOMER SERVICE
The Sandler Way

CUSTOMER SERVICE
The Sandler Way

48 Rules for Strategic Customer Care

ANNE MACKEIGAN

© 2015 Sandler Systems, Inc. All rights reserved.

Reproduction, modification, storage in a retrieval system or retransmission, in any form or by any means, electronic, mechanical or otherwise, is strictly prohibited without the prior written permission of Sandler Systems, Inc.

S Sandler Training (with design), Sandler, and Sandler Selling System are registered service marks of Sandler Systems, Inc.

Because the English language lacks a generic singular pronoun that indicates both genders, we have used the masculine pronouns for the sake of style, readability, and brevity. This material applies to both men and women.

Paperback: 978-0-692-46769-5
E-book: 978-0-692-46770-1

I dedicate this book to Eldon, my partner in business, and in life, who could not be more encouraging and supportive; to our daughters Kate and Megan, who taught me that every job is an important job and that bringing everything you have to those jobs assures success in life; and finally, to the countless frontline service providers I worked with in Sandler® training programs over the years who devoured useful information, were willing to try new methods, and generously shared their wisdom with me.

Contents

FOREWORD xi

INTRODUCTION xiii

    What Do We Mean by "Strategic Customer Care"? xviii

**CHAPTER 1: Sandler Rules for Customer-Service Hiring:
The Goldilocks Principle** 1

    1. Check for a Bias toward Action 3
    2. Check for a Strong Sense of Personal Responsibility 6
    3. Check for Process Orientation 9
    4. Check for a Relationship Focus 11
    5. Check for the Ability to Question and Qualify 15
    6. Measure Persistence and Armor around *No* 18
    7. Check for an Ability to "Read" a Situation 19
    8. Check for a Low Need for Approval 22
    9. Check for Strong Empathy 23
    10. Check for Manners and Etiquette 27
    Summary: Hiring 29

**CHAPTER 2: Sandler Rules for Training:
A Building Process for Productivity** 31

    Initial Training 32

Second Level Training............................33
Senior Level Training............................35
Ongoing Reinforcement Training 35

CHAPTER 3: Initial Training............................37

11. Train for Product Knowledge....................37
12. Train on Internal Systems and Partners 39
13. Set Clear Customer-Service Expectations 41

CHAPTER 4: Second Level Training........................43

14. Train for Basic Communication....................43
15. Train for Questioning and Listening 46
16. Train for Dealing with Difficult People..................50

CHAPTER 5: Senior Level Training........................55

17. Train for Reading People 55
18. Train for Finding Sales Opportunities..................57
19. Train Assertiveness, Not Aggressiveness...............60

CHAPTER 6: Ongoing Reinforcement Training..............65

20. Continue to Train Advanced Communication Skills.......65

CHAPTER 7: Sandler Rules for Process 69

21. Create Service Processes Based on
    What Customers Really Want........................71
22. Keep Your Processes Simple........................73
23. Have a Management Process........................76
24. Have a Process for Failure..........................79
25. Build Flexibility into Every Process....................82
26. Process the Detailed Grunt Work....................84
27. Have a Process for Problem Resolution 86
28. Have a Process to Win Back Ghosts 87
29. Have a Process for Continuous Improvement 90

CHAPTER 8: Sandler Rules for Finding Sales Opportunities . . 95

   30. Expect Resistance and Meet It with an Attitude Shift 98

   31. Use the Helping Approach to Growing Business 100

   32. Selling Is Something You Do with a Customer,
       Not to a Customer 103

   33. Understand the Value of One Customer 106

   34. Teach an Outbound Calling Process, Not a Script 109

   35. Become an Opportunity Finder 111

   36. Make Time for Business Development 113

   37. Sell Value, Not Price 117

   38. Check for Icebergs 120

   39. Stop Up-Selling; Instead, Extreme Up-Serve 122

CHAPTER 9: Sandler Rules for Up-Serving 125

   40. Make Customer Service Job Number One 126

   41. Sweat the Small Stuff 129

   42. Encourage Ownership 130

   43. To Keep Your Customers, Treat Them Like
       You Don't Have Them Yet 132

   44. Do More Than You're Paid For 135

   45. Fix Problems before They Happen 137

   46. Allow Customers to Ring the Bell 139

   47. Keep in Touch to Keep Relationships 140

   48. Engage Customers on an Emotional Level 142

EPILOGUE 145

   Changing Times 147

   The Future of Customer Experience 148

FOREWORD

It's quite common for clients to tell us, "We use the Sandler System for our whole company, not just the sales team." This book is a welcome reminder that David Sandler's breakthrough system of human interaction carries the power to transform the entire organization, and particularly those parts of it that interact directly with the customer.

Customer service has always been an important element of business strategy, but it's hard to imagine a time when it was more important than it is today. We live in an era when customer opinions not only matter deeply to the bottom line, but can radically transform the position of just about any business in very short order. A video testimonial from a happy customer can go viral within 24 hours and open up vast horizons of new opportunities for your company and everyone associated with it. By the same token, a mishandled exchange with a cranky customer can also build up an instant, deeply motivated army of followers on Facebook or any of a dozen other platforms, and can permanently damage your market potential – or even your company's existence.

In such an environment, it's important to bear in mind that everyone in your organization is, ultimately, part of the customer experience. It's also worth remembering that your company's customer service plan is only as strong as its weakest link. Anne MacKeigan's repositioning of the classic Sandler Selling System® methodology into a world-class customer care program is an essential resource for leaders and teams who understand, as all the best-in-class operations do, that superior customer service isn't something that gets added on after the sale closes. It's something that's built-in from the beginning of the relationship.

David H. Mattson
President and CEO, Sandler Training

INTRODUCTION

I rarely sleep well when I'm catching an early flight the next morning.

One night I found myself awake at 4 A.M. I posted my favorite battle cry on my Facebook page: "Be the kind of woman who, when your feet hit the floor in the morning, the devil says, 'Oh crap, she's up!'"

By 5:30 A.M., I was at the airport striving to be that woman, but I found it wasn't easy. The attendant handed me a boarding pass without a seat number—a sure sign that my flight had been oversold and I was not a winner of the seat lottery. Sitting at the gate, my next update said: "I'm headed to Baltimore to do a talk on customer service, and I can't even get out of my own airport without my blood pressure spiking like the dot-coms in the 80s."

Floods of sympathetic "likes" and "comments" appeared. Within moments, my update was followed by this answer from the airline: "Overselling flights is standard industry practice." Was this supposed to make me feel better?

Half an hour later, the gate agent appeared, grim-faced and steely-eyed. I was the first in line, ready to do battle; willing to say or do anything to get on my flight. But as I looked into the gate agent's face, I caught myself. What I saw was not her, but the people who had put this situation into action. I saw the board room table where the VP of sales told the group, "We have to oversell every flight; we can't afford not to." I saw the HR manager who was again refused additional hires and training, knowing that his front lines were under-staffed and stressed. I saw the customer experience manager being outvoted again in favor of saving money. I saw the operations manager who struggled trying to make the systems work more smoothly. And, I saw the final decision maker who made a tough call based on the numbers. The woman in front of me did not make the decision to oversell flights, but it was her job to do battle with me and the four people in line behind me.

Further, it was her first flight of the day. She likely had four or five more flights that were overbooked that day with four or five more people on each flight. It was her job to stand and defend other people's policies, negotiate settlements, calm frayed nerves, restore relationships—and do it well. Could I do that? I doubted it. I pictured her going home that night to her family, tired and brittle from a day of battle, burnout a distinct possibility.

What would be the upside of making this gate agent feel worse about the situation? Any exchange between the two of us now could only be helped by supporting, not persecuting, her. Frontline service providers are often blamed for company policy, lack of training, poor hiring practices and an internal system that makes it hard for customers to do business.

So, I smiled at this customer service warrior and said, "Please do what you can to get me on this flight. Thanks."

She gave me a grateful smile, and I was the first of the waiting group to get a seat assignment. When I did post a review of the situation at the end of the day, it was in full support of the service representative and included pointed enquiries about the company's policies.

Think how differently this story might have ended. What if I had been confrontational with this airline employee, as any number of customers might have chosen to do? Our discussion could have escalated to an ugly scene that 250 other passengers overheard. Some onlookers may have tweeted it, put it on Facebook or related the story to friends and family. I even had a reporter friend who was doing an article on airline policy on overselling flights. She would have loved an interview about a conflict I had with an airline representative. That negative encounter could have reached tens of thousands, perhaps hundreds of thousands of people.

Here's another story that illustrates how many customer-service stories these days do indeed have lives of their own.

In a suburban mall in Oregon in 2013, a 14-year-old girl was shamed out of a chain store when the clerk told her she was "too fat" to shop there and asked her to leave. The story not only went viral on the Internet but was picked up by print media across the country and around the world. We've seen this happen increasingly in the last few years. One employee, one encounter, one customer, but hundreds of thousands of ears hearing the story.

The outrage that this story produced on the Internet is indicative of technology's ability to "get the word out" lightning fast to millions of readers. The millions spent on marketing, presentation, product mix and overheads can be damaged by poor customer service. One negative experience like this young girl had, and you have a public relations crisis on your hands.

This book and its 48 Rules for Strategic Customer Care give

you the guidelines you need to make intelligent investments in customer care—and create and sustain a working culture that's built on the belief that the customer not only matters, but is the only reason your organization exists.

The kinds of investments I'll be asking you, the company or team leader, to make—investments not just of money, but of time, attention, and political capital—fall into five specific categories. Superior customer service is a puzzle you and your organization must put together, a puzzle with pieces that include:

1. Good **hiring** practices.
2. Proper **training** on more than just product information.
3. A seamless, customer-friendly **process** for every aspect of a customer's journey with your company, including well-thought-out policies to ease every step along the way.
4. An employee-friendly process for developing new business **sales opportunities** when they arise.
5. Clearly communicated expectations regarding both sales and **up-serving,** which means looking beyond the customer's immediate need to the reason behind it.

Each of these five categories is a section of this book, and each section contains Rules for Strategic Customer Care relevant to that section, based on the teachings and principles of our company's founder, David Sandler.

WHAT DO WE MEAN BY "STRATEGIC CUSTOMER CARE"?

At Sandler, we believe that customer care is not about putting up a poster, memorizing a script or reciting a slogan. We believe customer care must be strategic. This means both identifying long-term or overall goals for customer care and laying out how those goals will be achieved. Building your business culture around strategic customer care means identifying the tactical, calculated, pragmatic steps that ensure your customers' good experience in the short term and their loyalty in the long term.

Customer relationships are like marriages: You want to build them for the long term. If they have a good foundation, open communication, mutual respect, and good intentions, they can weather almost any storm. Care for your customers today, in anticipation of the time when the relationship may experience some strain, and your customers will know from experience that they can trust you to make it right.

CHAPTER 1

Sandler Rules for Customer-Service Hiring: The Goldilocks Principle

Before you hire a customer-care provider, you must know what is important to find. Create a checklist of "must haves" and "don't compromises." If you're going to be picky, obsessive and unreasonably selective about anything, make it about the people you put in front of, or on the phone with, your customers. Disappointment, frustration and regret may occur if you don't check before you hire.

Check that your candidate:

1. Has a bias toward action.
2. Has a strong sense of personal responsibility.
3. Can balance process orientation with an ability to step outside the process.

4. Focuses on building business relationships.
5. Has an ability to question and qualify.
6. Demonstrates persistence and armor around *no*.
7. Has an ability to quickly "read" a situation.
8. Has a low need for approval.
9. Has strong empathy.
10. Demonstrates good manners and etiquette.

There is no one perfect description for a customer-care provider. A law office customer-care provider may have different job requirements than one at a call center. Think about the results you want, and write the job description accordingly. However, the above ten factors apply to almost every business-to-customer interaction and every customer-service provider.

Every strength has the potential to be a weakness if it comes in too much quantity. Good detail-oriented employees can get so hung up on details that they never complete a task. The great relationship builder may never get around to asking for the customer's business. On the other hand, too little of a competency can also be a problem. Too little detail orientation and things are missed. Too little relationship orientation and the customer feels neglected and emotionally detached. Remember Goldilocks's criteria? Not too hot and not too cold? Make sure your candidate strikes the appropriate balance.

1. CHECK FOR A BIAS TOWARD ACTION

If you want to measure productivity in your customer-care providers, measure their bias toward action before you hire. Taking action is a quality that says, "I must do something, so I'll quickly assess the situation, decide on a path, and do something myself." Rather than wait for the customer to call back, a bias toward action says to reach out to the customer first. A bias toward action is the proactive ingredient in customer care.

> Julie had been promoted from production to her customer-service job by being friendly, reliable and well-liked by staff. Her first week on the phones, her supervisor was quite sure he had made a good decision. Listening in on her calls, he could see that people took to her right away.
>
> While covering lunch breaks, Julie got a call from Greg, a customer with a reputation as demanding and gruff. "Where's Bob?" Greg barked.
>
> "Bob's out sick today. This is Julie. Is there some way I can help you?"
>
> "I need my usual Thursday order a day early, and I need it shipped by overnight courier today. Think you can handle that, Julie?" he asked sarcastically.
>
> "Absolutely," said Julie. "Thanks for the call." Julie felt good that she could make Greg, such a difficult customer, happy.

After she hung up, however, Julie realized that she had been so intimidated by his attitude that she had not checked any of the things she should have: What was his usual order? Did the warehouse have the items in stock now? Could they pack it today? What time did the last courier do pickups? Could they even deliver overnight?

Julie knew by the feeling in her stomach that while she had made Greg happy for the moment, she had set herself up for problems by not asking those questions. If she went to accounting to get copies of Greg's Thursday order, she'd have to leave the phones unattended. She decided to wait and ask her supervisor when she returned from lunch in an hour. She didn't want to call Greg back, risking his wrath, to confirm the information. He'd think she was an idiot for not knowing already.

When at last she had someone to ask procedures, she had missed her window of time to either process the order or to call Greg back and explain why they couldn't deliver. Her supervisor was upset, the customer was upset and Julie felt like a failure—all because she didn't go ahead and right the situation herself from the beginning.

There are a number of reasons why customer-service providers might not take action right away. Sometimes they're afraid of someone being angry with them; sometimes they're afraid of making a mistake. Perhaps they simply reason that waiting is a better option than making the wrong move. Whatever the reason, the customer sees it as neglect—they don't really care about the *why*.

Had Julie gone ahead and called Greg back, she may have found him to be helpful or not helpful. But whatever his reaction, it would have been better than not warning him of the possibility of not getting his product on time. Julie chose inaction when she should have braved the consequences and picked up the phone. Having a bias toward doing something, no matter what the consequences, is always preferable to doing nothing and hoping things will work out. They seldom do.

In hiring Julie, HR put a premium on likeability rather than a bias toward action. It's great to be liked, but it's more important to be respected. Asking all the questions would likely have given Greg a more secure feeling that he would have the product as promised. If he couldn't have it on time, he would have had more choices about what to do next.

Employees who can follow instructions are fine; they are certainly easy to manage. In customer service, however, it helps to have people who can see where problems might arise and stop them before they happen. You want employees who can do more than react to a situation. If you don't hire for a bias toward action, you may get an employee with a default setting that believes, "I did my best." A candidate with a more entrepreneurial attitude would be unwilling to stop until the problem was acted upon and solved. Entrepreneurs go beyond their limits to a solution and can quickly connect the dots between customer needs and their company's products, services and solutions.

Going beyond prescribed limits to achieve a customer-satisfying solution is a company-mandated culture. If customer-service providers are encouraged to do this, if they're told that creative solutions are encouraged, then the result is a customer-happy culture. If the providers are only permitted to follow the rulebook, you can expect outcomes like Julie's. If they're encouraged to push the limits, on the other hand, the result will be better outcomes.

If you do check for proactivity, problem solving and problem finding before you hire, you should also provide a working environment where these traits are valued, not shunned. Nothing can demotivate a problem solver faster than being told, "We've always done it this way," and then being ignored. If you're going to the trouble to seek out intelligent employees, give them the opportunity and freedom to solve problems as well as to present alternatives. Don't shut them down or throttle them with rules and regulations that don't enable their strengths.

2. CHECK FOR A STRONG SENSE OF PERSONAL RESPONSIBILITY

A high level of personal responsibility in a customer-care provider is not alone a predictor of success. But a lack of taking personal responsibility can frustrate customers, make them feel neglected and can certainly harm relationships.

At a fast food restaurant, I noticed that the teenaged waitresses would immediately turn to carefully cleaning and prepping their area the moment there was no one waiting in line. Likewise, as soon as someone approached the counter, one would pop up immediately and ask to be of service. The only time they spoke to each other was to ask a business-related question. There was no filling time chatting about their day; they were completely focused on serving customers and creating a clean, inviting environment. These teenagers obviously took pride in their jobs, their workplace and their role. Anyone can learn to wipe a table, but the internal motivation to actively make the workplace better is much harder to instill. Taking responsibility for your work area, your customers and their problems is key.

When problems arise, blame is a useless tool. Having the maturity to say, "I didn't create this problem, but I will be the one to fix it," is the sign of a great customer-care provider. Customer-care providers with this characteristic will make statements like:

- "I am so sorry this situation occurred. Can I help to make it right?"
- "We hate to see these mistakes happen. I'm here to ensure it gets straightened out."
- "I can see this has really upset you. Fortunately, I'm the one to see this gets fixed."

These statements don't deflect blame. They don't accuse or defend. They simply acknowledge that the customer has an issue and take responsibility for finding a solution.

In interviews, candidates will tell you they love to serve customers, that caring is their top priority and that they take their jobs to heart. Six months down the road, you may see that their job is a means to pay their rent and nothing more. Internal motivation can be encouraged, but it's a difficult thing to create when it's not there in the beginning. Why make your job harder by not weeding out those who lack a strong sense of personal responsibility?

Personal responsibility means taking a job seriously, no matter how big or small. It means doing more than you are paid to do. It means caring about doing a great job, whether someone is watching you or not. Those who want to progress in their career path within a company understand that taking personal responsibility for the job they have now is the way to earn that right. Driving a company forward means that every employee has taken personal responsibility toward achieving excellence. It means taking personal responsibility in solving customer problems, not passing them off to someone else. It means taking pride in the job, the company and one's own personal performance.

Assess and interview with a view to a candidate's level of personal responsibility. There is a great distance between shifting blame and sidestepping responsibility and being burdened or overly responsible to the point of paralysis. Use the Goldilocks Principle. Make sure your candidates strike the appropriate balance.

3. CHECK FOR PROCESS ORIENTATION

Like the other areas of a company—the warehouse, the accounting department, shipping—customer care is a process. In fact, it typically involves a number of processes, such as incoming order processing, returns and re-stocking, setting up new accounts and solving customer problems. If a customer-care candidate does not already have a process orientation, it will be an uphill battle to instill one.

> John had been the supervisor of customer care for over ten years, but he had never had an employee make as many mistakes as Brian. While Brian was a wonderful person, a bright light in the company and well-liked by his customers, keeping him on track with company processes was a constant challenge and was sometimes disruptive to other employees. Worse yet, customers were experiencing delays in getting their orders because Brian didn't seem capable of following the bouncing ball. To John it seemed so simple, but Brian was constantly trying to reinvent an existing process that, if followed, already worked quite well. He would often ignore the new accounts process and send out stock before an account was approved. Customers loved it, but it often backfired by causing delays.
>
> John hated to admit it, but it looked like Brian was too scattered. He was not a good fit for the job. John couldn't think of any other area of the company that didn't have

processes to follow, so there was no better place for Brian to go. In the end, John had to release Brian from the company and wish him the best in his future.

Process orientation can be uncovered in both assessments and interview questions. Having this orientation serves to instill much-needed confidence in the customer. It creates a comfort level for the buyer, for the employee and for others in the company, ensuring that nothing is being missed. Good processes ensure smooth dealings with no unnecessary touchpoints, resulting in the best possible outcomes for you and your customers.

Too little process orientation can be troublesome, as the story above demonstrates, but too much process orientation can also be a problem. If a customer-care employee is afraid to step off the process when a situation calls for it, he may become dogmatic and rigid. Rigidity in following processes can cause as many problems as not following processes at all. Employees need to know where the boundaries are as well as company expectations as to when they should use their own judgment to cross those lines.

Carl had never had a shipment go so wrong, so fast. A new product had been shipped for a grand opening, and it was missing and untrackable. The customer, one of Carl's best, was beside himself with worry. Carl's boss was in an important client meeting, so Carl made a quick decision. He offered to leave work, pack a replacement shipment in the back of his car and drive the two hours to the customer's workplace. It would not be there for the opening bell, but at least the customer could tell clients when it would arrive. The customer was ecstatic. Carl knew he was pushing the boundaries and completely disrupting his and his colleagues' workday, but this customer was in a spot and he made the decision to fix it. He believed his supervisor would have done the same. He was right.

Knowing when to subvert the process is as important as sticking to it, as a general rule. Carl's customer would not soon forget this demonstration of up-service (service so excellent that it inspires the customer to expand the relationship with the seller).

Again, the Goldilocks Principle applies. Blind adherence to process is too hard. No process at all is too soft. Find the balance for a customer experience that's just right.

4. CHECK FOR A RELATIONSHIP FOCUS

Check before you hire for a candidate's overall people skills.

The best people skills that candidates will ever employ are in the interview situation as they try to win a position. If they don't capture you there, do you really want them in front of your valuable customers?

In my hiring practice, I have a checklist for telephone interviews—my first hoop for qualifying candidates. Candidates must score a minimum of 27 out of a possible 30 points to be invited to submit a resume. A critical part of the phone interview is people skills. Candidates are awarded points for how they come across on the telephone. Below are some of the criteria I use to evaluate candidates.

Do they pull me in? This is a rapport-building reference that includes using my name, employing good listening skills and showing a respectful amount of familiarity, politeness, good grammar and focus. In short, I have my radar switched on to something called "manners." I am listening for phrases like:

- "Thanks for taking my call, Anne."
- "Do you have time right now to chat?"
- "I appreciate you taking the time to talk today."
- "Can I share something with you, Anne?"
- "Anne, will I have an opportunity to meet with you at some point?"
- "Can you help me understand the process from here?"

When I hear these things from a candidate I write an immediate "Wow!" or "Good!" or "Schedule Interview" across the top of a telephone screen sheet.

How do they make me feel? Believe it or not, I often feel completely frustrated after completing a telephone screen. This is often because:

- The candidate wasn't prepared and didn't know the content of the job listing itself. This makes me feel like I have to hand-hold and fill in information the candidate should already know.

- The candidate obviously wasn't listening, as proved by an inability to answer questions I asked.
- The candidate talked randomly about himself and wasn't focused.
- The candidate used poor grammar or inappropriate language. This is cause for an immediate "no" written on his telephone screen sheet.
- The candidate asked self-serving questions about money, hours, breaks or vacation time. These questions are important, but the time for them is later in the process and not in an initial qualifying conversation.

Hiring employees well-suited to customer care will result in great customer relationships, internal motivation of frontline employees, less burnout and higher customer retention. Remember that there is little chance that the quality of your customer service can exceed the quality of the people who deliver that service. Hire the best, and then train them to your highest standards.

> My interview with Henry was going well. The service desk position for which I was hiring required a broad understanding of air-conditioning controls, and Henry seemed to have a thorough background. His answers to my questions reflected a high degree of attention to detail, accuracy and care when filling orders. In fact, I had never seen such a high assessment score on accuracy of orders filled.

As I began to ask him about his soft skills, the reason Henry may have been looking for a job became clearer. He described his job as a long list of tasks that he performed daily. I asked, "Tell me about your customer base, Henry. Who typically shows up at your counter in the run of a day?" Henry seemed puzzled, and struggled to answer the question. "I mean," I continued, "tell me about a typical customer that you've had for a while."

"They're HVAC techs who need controls," he answered, still puzzled.

"You know, Henry, in my experience, HVAC techs are a pretty friendly bunch. They like to chat about last night's game, or about new products, or issues they're having with equipment. Do you find the same thing?"

"No," replied Henry, "they just want what they want and that's it."

My guess was that Henry wanted to get them what they wanted and that was all. Just like his conversation with me, he wanted to get the task done and not waste time on idle chat.

My problem was that the "idle chat" that occurs between customer and customer-service provider is often what builds long-term, loyal customers. Without it, customers are vulnerable to the competition where they do receive a friendly smile and warm welcome.

I will always choose a good balance of technical expertise

and relationship skills over just one or the other. But in my experience, a higher level of technical expertise can be developed over time. It's more challenging to train someone to be more interpersonal.

Customer care is a face-to-face, brain-to-brain activity. Is it possible that some of your frontline people are not suited to dealing directly with customers? Maybe they're great with one-on-one conversations, but fail to follow up with customers and deliver what they promise? Too high a relationship focus, and the customer-care provider may waste valuable time on personal chat or frustrate the customer by not getting down to business quickly enough. Too low a relationship focus, and the customer may feel detached or neglected. A relationship focus has to be just right to ensure not only that an emotional connection is made with a customer, but that business is done and problems are solved in a timely manner.

5. CHECK FOR THE ABILITY TO QUESTION AND QUALIFY

One descriptor of customer-care providers is "professional communicator." It is their job to gather information from prospects and customers, to fully understand their needs and to recommend or sell services or products that are a good fit. Sometimes it is a very simple transaction in that you are duplicating a past order. But more often, customers don't know exactly what they need or want. An ability to question and qualify is key. Great questioning and qualifying comes both from innate abilities and from trained techniques. One of those innate abilities is curiosity.

Curiosity is a natural tendency to wonder what is behind a customer's request—and it's a valuable asset. The questions are simple: "Can I ask you how you'll be using that widget?" "Do you expect to be taking this vehicle on long trips, or will you simply be using it to get around town?" Curiosity indicates the customer-care provider is thinking of the big picture and is truly trying to fit the right product to the customer's use and expectation. Thinking of the big picture on behalf of the customer is a proactive process. If you sell a customer the first widget he asks for, you may end up with an unhappy customer.

Wendy decided to solve a problem in her government office with a roped off area to create orderly customer lines, like banks. She visited a supplier and told them she wanted the stands and rope to create this area. She sent a truck to pick up the stands and rope. When she went to put them in place, Wendy realized there was no way to attach the ropes to the stands. When she phoned the supplier, their representative said, "Oh, you need the O-rings that clip into the stands for that. You didn't mention you needed those."

One or two questions would have solved a problem that necessitated another trip to the supplier and resulted in a disgruntled customer. Experience should have revealed that most people who want stands and ropes need the entire package. Do you think this is a basic, common sense behavior that everyone does? You may be surprised at how often customer-care providers give only exactly what is asked for and don't take the next step.

Learning to ask questions that will match the customer's needs to your products and services is key. Having the internal motivation and curiosity to ask those questions is an indication of the proactivity required in customer care.

The final upside of asking questions is engaging the customer. Conversations should be relationship-building, not simply transactional. The better questions you ask a customer, the more likely you are to hear about his roadblocks—the challenges that clog his days and keep him awake at night. These are the kinds of emotional conversations that can differentiate you from competitors who only skim the surface of customer needs.

It also ensures that there is no attempt at "mind reading" or assumptions that you know what the customer needs because he sounds like other customers you've had. Mind reading can lead to mutual mystification—the belief that you know when you honestly don't. You wind up delivering the wrong product or service or simply frustrate the customer.

Questioning and qualifying can be evident in both assessment results and interview results. Watch for what candidates ask you. Are they engaging you in conversation or simply answering what you asked?

Striking the balance between assuming you already understand a customer's needs and overburdening the customer with irrelevant questions is key. The sweet spot is likely closer to more well-developed questions than no questions.

6. MEASURE PERSISTENCE AND ARMOR AROUND *NO*

Often customer-care people give up too soon on a prospect or customer when in the sales mode. One thing to check new candidates for is an ability to avoid or resist stalls and objections. Customer-care providers often eschew the perceived aggressiveness and persistence of the stereotypical salesperson. This leads them to the opposite approach of asking a direct question and giving up at the first sign of resistance. This behavior can be bad news for the customer.

> Michelle had been in customer care for four years and was an outstanding relationship builder. She was singled out because of her great relationships to contact customers about the new product line the company had recently acquired and was instructed to get as many demos lined up as she could from a list of 300 top customers. Michelle was reluctant. It was one thing to help customers when they called, but she certainly wasn't a salesperson. Being asked to do this was unfair; this was a job for the sales department.
>
> After her first ten calls, Michelle went to her supervisor and explained that no one was interested in these products, and there was probably no point calling the rest of the list. Disappointed in Michelle, her supervisor took back the list

and told Michelle to forget it. Michelle felt terrible. She felt she had failed the company, her boss and herself.

The problem was that the company was making a classic mistake. It was akin to asking a person with no legs to carry you. In other words, they sent an unprepared, ill-equipped person to do a job she wasn't ready for with disastrous results. It was unfair.

Ensuring an employee has a tough skin and has a process for approaching an outbound call is key. They also need to have the right level of persistence and tenacity, an ability to empathize with customers and a very low need for validation from others. Making sure a customer-care employee has the tools, training and ability to handle the job is only fair. It is one reason for a lack of employee engagement and resulting high attrition rates. Burnout is a natural result of employees being asked to do what they have not been hired and trained to do. No matter whether they leave the company or they stay and become disengaged, the result is typically a poor one for everyone involved.

Hiring for resistance to stalls and objections can be achieved through the assessment and interview processes. Too little, and the employee will resist doing the required behaviors; too high, and they may be offensive to customers. Applying the Goldilocks Principle ensures the best outcomes.

7. CHECK FOR AN ABILITY TO "READ" A SITUATION

Check your candidates' insight and understanding before you hire. Are they "people smart"? Part of customer care is a heightened ability to read people and to understand why they act the way they do. In order to accomplish this, one must become a student of human behavior. Socially intelligent people are skilled at reading body language, tonality and particularly the emotions of others. They pick up on the emotions of customers immediately, whether in person or on the phone. And, they react appropriately.

While for one person saying, "What a great job you did on that Acme account. Congratulations!" would be a natural verbal "pat on the back," for another, it might come across as, "OK. What happens next?" The person is not trying to downplay the other person's achievements; he's simply displaying his communication style.

> Everyone in the office knew when Emily had a situation on her hands. She often handled the more difficult, escalated customers who were very upset or emotional in some way, and they knew when she was doing so because her voice would become very calm and she would speak much more slowly. Emily seemed to know how to handle situations that would have stressed others or hooked them into a negative state of mind. Emily's calm questions, caring tonality and focus on the customer never failed to calm and resolve. The outcomes were typically win/win.
>
> Once a coworker asked Emily her secret. Here's what she said: "I believe that everyone I meet each day is fighting a battle that I can't see and I know nothing about. Maybe they

have a sick child at home; maybe their company is in financial trouble. I don't know what it is, but I picture everyone as having something that's troubling them. I approach them as though they have bigger problems than this immediate one, and I can be a bright spot in their day by solving it."

What Emily knows is that not everything is about her. She doesn't take things personally. She has a deep understanding of people, why they act the way they do and the pressures that some are feeling. She's not afraid to explore those feelings and to help.

At Sandler, we use a number of tools to help us become better "readers." One of these is the DISC assessment tool that describes a four-quadrant model of preferred behaviors. First, a person identifies his own style, and then he becomes aware of styles that differ from his own and how better to communicate with those styles.

Next is the neuro-linguistic programming process, through which we identify how a person likes to both communicate and take in information from the world. Is the person visual, auditory or kinesthetic? These insights help us to read people's preferences as well as their learning styles.

Finally, we use transactional analysis to identify people's ego state at a particular moment. This gives us some emotional cues as to where an individual is at any given point in time.

Coming to a customer-care job with an innate ability to recognize your customers' emotional states and what they need emotionally is a big plus. Bringing human insight to a business situation is incredibly helpful. Things are not always black and white. In order to build the kind of loyal customer relationships you need and want, you must show compassion and understanding. Knowing when and how to offer support is part of being able to read situations and people. Too little of that, and the company and service appear dehumanized. Too much reading can appear invasive and too personal. Just the right amount of understanding of human nature and emotional situations will set relationships on the right course.

8. CHECK FOR A LOW NEED FOR APPROVAL

If it is more important to customer-care providers to be liked by the customer than to be respected and trusted, then they are opening themselves, their customers and their company up to a host of potential problems.

> Frank interviewed new candidates for a customer-care position and immediately connected with one. Julie was extremely likeable and made him laugh several times. He could picture her easily fitting into the productive group that was his customer-care team. He decided to give her the position.
>
> Within weeks, he began to notice problems. Julie would over-promise, and he would overhear her on the phone trying to placate upset customers. She would rarely say "no" to helping coworkers, but he would find her own productivity

slipping because of it. She would spend far too much time with customers while others were waiting for service. When a customer gave her pushback on price, she would constantly give in or rush to her supervisor to ask for a price break.

Julie's problem was a high need to be liked. She wanted that approval; she was looking to get her needs met in an inappropriate manner. She was afraid that drawing boundaries with customers would send them running to the competition. While it is nice when customers like you, is it not more important that they find you effective, efficient, trustworthy and pleasant?

Of course I don't mean to demonize the ability to be empathetic and customer focused; those are necessary traits of any good customer-care provider. But like too much exercise can have negative effects, too much empathy can cross the line to sympathy and too much customer focus can be detrimental to the company. Again, there must always be a balance. In the case of needing to be liked, the Goldilocks Principle applies. There's a position somewhere between "desperate to please" and "cold and uncaring." The Goldilocks Principle means establishing boundaries and being businesslike. It means being friendly but not necessarily best friends.

9. CHECK FOR STRONG EMPATHY

Empathy is the ability to experience, feel and understand what others are experiencing without actually experiencing it yourself. When you display deep empathy toward others, their defensive energy depletes and their positive energy rises. Without a display of empathy, customer-service providers are facing an uphill battle with the negative energy that emanates from upset customers. Customers prefer you to show them that you care before you show them what you know.

Whether empathy is something you are born with or it is taught through socialization as a child, it is a key ingredient in successful customer-care professionals.

It was 4:30 P.M. on a beautiful summer afternoon. Everyone at the company had either left for the day or was attending the company deep-sea fishing competition. The only one left in the office was the new receptionist.

Only two weeks on the job and barely 22 years old, Ruth was excited to be trusted to lock up for the first time. Gathering her things to leave, the phone rang. She set her things down again and answered.

"Where's Ted Moore? Let me talk to him right now!" boomed a voice through the phone.

A quick check of the call display told her it was Mr. Vincent, the firm's #1 customer. She hesitated for a moment and with a rising knot in her stomach, replied, "I'm sorry, Mr. Vincent. Mr. Moore is unavailable at the moment. This sounds very important, though. Is there some way I might help you?"

Ruth had no idea if she could help or not, but she did the one thing she knew she could do well—listen and empathize. Mr. Vincent proceeded to rant about a promised shipment being late and causing delays for his client. She patiently waited until he had blown off steam.

"I can see why you're frustrated, Mr. Vincent. We hate to keep our clients waiting, too. I'm going to repack that order now and drive it over there myself. Will someone be there to receive it in about 20 minutes?"

"Oh, don't do that," Mr. Vincent replied, now calmed down. "Just make sure it's here by 9:00 A.M. Monday, and we'll chalk it up to experience."

Ruth apologized again and reassured him he would not be disappointed on Monday. She would personally see that it got done.

First thing Monday morning, Ted Moore got a call again from Mr. Vincent, this time thanking him for the wonderful job Ruth had done and how much he appreciated getting his product so early on Monday.

Ruth had overcome shyness, her worry about her own inexperience and her fears around angry people and had allowed herself to simply empathize with her customer. Her innate desire to help people was more than enough for this important client. She not only ameliorated his anger, but she made a personal connection.

Test for empathy in the hiring process through your questions. For example, you can ask:

- "Tell me about a time when you had to deal with a very upset customer."
- "What would you do with a frustrated customer who was at fault for providing the wrong shipping address but complained about the lateness of the shipment?"

What you're looking for is how the customer-service provider addressed the customer's emotion, not the physical solution. You want to hear things like: "Well, first I listened carefully to his story," or "I let him rant a bit and told him how sorry I was that he was upset," or "I knew it wasn't my fault, but I also saw in what a difficult situation this had put him." That's empathy.

Empathy has the power to change a confrontational situation to a relationship-building one. It is the proof of concern and caring that an upset customer needs. It diffuses tense situations, lowers defenses and allows for problem solving to happen. Like all strengths, too much empathy can become a weakness. Low empathy may show as impersonal, cold and uninterested; too much empathy may reveal itself as overly sensitive and emotional or smarmy and fake. Empathy projects sensitivity and a willingness to help others through action. In other words, empathetic people identify with their customers and then move to problem solving through action. The right amount of empathy connects you to your customers in a way that builds trust and loyalty.

10. CHECK FOR MANNERS AND ETIQUETTE

As Anglican clergyman and novelist Laurence Stern said, "Respect for ourselves guides our morals. Respect for others guides our manners." Treating people in a way that displays respect, care and consideration is the core of good manners. While they do not appear to be the priority they once were, good manners are invaluable in customer service, in business in general and in building relationships in all areas. Manners can help you have better relationships—both present and future.

Good manners are a two-sided tool; they not only convey respect to customers with whom you interact, but they also command respect from those people.

Kevin slipped out from behind the leasing counter. Keys in hand, he picked up the suitcase, opened the door and invited his customer to follow him. He led him through the parking lot, found the appropriate car and dropped the suitcase into the trunk. Handing him a map of the local area, Kevin bent down beside the customer as he settled into the rented car.

"Now, to exit the lot just bear left all the way out. Once on the highway, you're going to again bear left until you see the signs for the business park. Is there anything else I can do for you today, Mr. Smith? Remember, I'm Kevin, my card is attached to your contract and if you need anything, just call me directly."

This was Kevin's usual process. His coworkers typically

simply hand customers a set of keys, tell them the parking lot number of the car and thank them for renting from their company. They would kid Kevin about "working too hard" or "brown nosing," but Kevin was undeterred. Making that extra effort showed in his return-customer stats. *Besides*, thought Kevin, *it's just the right thing to do.*

A hiring interview is a small microcosm of life, and how someone acts in an interview is probably the height of his manners and etiquette. He isn't holding out to display his manners at another time; he's pouring it on for you—now. Here's what to look for:

- Saying, "Excuse me," "Please," and "Thank you."
- Offering, "Let me get the door for you," or "May I get the door for you?"
- Speaking slowly and precisely, with no slang or "fillers" ("uh," "er").
- Listening carefully, not interrupting or overriding another speaker and answering when asked. Talking when it's his turn.
- Knowing how to greet people in different circumstances. (Test this by having a surprise addition sit in on the interview to see how candidates politely introduce themselves and address the new person.)
- Sending thank-you follow-up notes. (If they do not contact you to thank you after an interview, it's a sign.)

Ask them to show you how they answer the phone. Phone etiquette is critical for anyone in customer service today. There are few positions that don't require at least some phone time.

Finally, watch how much candidates talk about themselves. Do they ramble on with stories that stray from the question asked? This may indicate a lack of awareness of the listener and a desire to hear themselves talk. I once asked a candidate for a three-minute thumbnail sketch of their background in customer care. When the candidate reached twenty minutes, I stopped him and thanked him for coming. This candidate either did not listen to the instructions or was unaware of the passage of time. Either way, he was not the kind of employee I would present to any of my clients.

One of the fortunate outcomes of having manners is that it contributes to a personal presence. Before you hire, check that your candidates are present and engaged in the moment, bring energy to the conversation and appear genuine. Personal presence is also evident in a candidate's listening skills and attentiveness to what you're saying.

SUMMARY: HIRING

Hiring is a science and an art. Having a clear job description is important, but equally important are the soft "people" skills that make a customer-service provider great. Those skills are much more challenging to instill after you hire. Avoid that challenge by checking for attitudes and behaviors before you hire. Hire for engagement and intensity. There is training for everything else.

CHAPTER 2

Sandler Rules for Training: A Building Process for Productivity

No one comes to a job 100 percent prepared for success. If you have done a good job in the hiring and assessment process, your people may arrive 60 to 70 percent ready. You must train for the other 30 percent. Too often customer-care training takes the form of "sit by me" sessions, where present employees are expected to pass along knowledge and experience. This feels like a shortcut to bringing new employees up to speed, but you may be unwittingly passing on undesirable attitudes, behaviors and techniques instead. If you want professional customer-care providers, wouldn't it make sense to invest in their knowledge, processes and interpersonal skills?

To paraphrase Zig Ziglar, you don't build a business; you build people, and they build the business.

There are four levels of training for customer-service employees.

INITIAL TRAINING	2ND LEVEL TRAINING	SENIOR TRAINING	ONGOING
• Product Information • Internal Systems and Partners • Customer Service Expectations	• Basic Communication • Questioning and Listening • Dealing with Difficult People	• Reading People • Sales Training and Opportunity Finding	• Advanced Communication Skills

INITIAL TRAINING

Like most jobs, the initial training is likely around product knowledge. Becoming familiar with products, services, internal processes, people, roles and expected outcomes is a monumental task. The expectation that employees can download information on the first pass and commit it to their long-term memory is unrealistic. A carefully constructed onboarding plan that shares information and expertise with a new employee over time is the sensible way to build product and company knowledge.

The second part of initial training must include technology training. The faster technology changes, the less comfortable some long-term employees may be. But the experience, knowledge, collective wisdom and relationships of those employees is too valuable to risk losing. Ensure that all employees stay current with technology upgrades through training. Confidence and motivation can erode over time if employees feel technology is leaving them behind.

In initial training, managing the expectations of new frontline employees on the service levels, sales functions, internal customers and expected outcomes is a process that should begin as early as the first interview. One early and crucial conversation sounds like this: "In our company, we have a culture of accountability. That means that the behaviors and expected outcomes are clearly defined, tracked and regularly reviewed by supervisors with employees. Have you experienced that kind of accountability before, and can you describe to me what that was like for you?"

Accountability is just one area that should be covered. In most companies, there is a common language, a common sales process, a dress code and an accounting system. All these make up the company culture and should be clearly communicated to new employees.

SECOND LEVEL TRAINING

The second level of training for new customer-care employees concerns communications. These employees can be thought of as professional communicators and therefore deserve support in ensuring good communication happens with both internal and external customers.

Listening and questioning techniques are basic to communication. Often a key disconnect in communications happens between the sales group (bringing business into the company) and customer service (keeping and growing that business). When there is a disconnect between those two groups, it is the customer who suffers. It could be opportunities or perhaps deadlines are missed. Whatever it is, it is bound to affect the customer directly. Better connection between sales and customer service is achieved through communication training.

The basic elements of communication are key. More issues arise due to miscommunication than for any other reason. Vague language, poor tonality and negative body language result in defensiveness, frustration and outright hostility. There is a language around customer care that is both nurturing and helpful, but not patronizing. It is businesslike but caring; it conveys confidence and empathy. For many, it does not come naturally—but it can be learned. It usually helps to have a systematic way to deal with difficult people and difficult situations.

Finally, understanding how different people communicate in different styles will help with a deeper understanding of themselves and how to adapt to others. Using tools like the DISC model, transactional analysis and neuro-linguistic programming will help in this area. Communications training sets the standards for how to treat each other, how to take people from Not-OK to OK, how to communicate your value, products and services and how to sell. It communicates how you feel about your customers and influences how they feel about you.

SENIOR LEVEL TRAINING

Many employers look for behavior change in their frontline employees—better sales techniques that result in better outcomes, upgraded communication styles that avoid conflict, or more engagement and work ethic. These are behaviors that can be quantified and tracked and that significantly affect company revenues. These important behaviors should be reinforced through constant upgrading in sales training.

Behavior change takes time. It begins with an awareness that leads to knowledge. Knowledge leads to adaptation, which then leads to building skills—also known as visible behavior change. This means changes don't occur overnight and training must be ongoing and reinforced.

ONGOING REINFORCEMENT TRAINING

At 86 years of age, the brilliant writer, scientist, artist and philosopher Michelangelo was quoted as saying, "*Ancaro imparo*" ("I am still learning"). To be engaged in their jobs, employees need to be challenged and growing. Give them opportunities to learn, improve and grow as employees and as people. Continuing to train employees will grow self-esteem, confidence, skills and more consistent behaviors. No one is ever "done."

CHAPTER 3

Initial Training

11. TRAIN FOR PRODUCT KNOWLEDGE

The first days and weeks on a new job in a new company can be overwhelming for a customer-service employee. There is so much to absorb, and there are so many details and systems to keep straight. Without a carefully constructed onboarding plan that takes place over weeks (if not months, depending on your company), a new employee can have a difficult time.

Nowhere in the organization is it more critical to know your products and services, your marketplace and your industry than on the front lines. If you are looking to staff your front line with those who can build trust relationships, these must be built on a broad understanding of three things.

1. First, the ability to make the connection between the customers' needs and the products and services you sell is job number one for frontline employees. They must have a thorough understanding of your products and services or be able to quickly access additional information. This can be learned through a combination of on-the-job training, job shadowing with experts, reading, online resources—wherever your resources are located. Lunch-and-learns conducted by different departments will help them understand new product development, changes in products and services and future plans. Naturally, the longer employees stay on the job, the deeper their knowledge and understanding.
2. Next, understanding the marketplace is key. Who is your target customer? Who is your competition, and what makes you different from them? What are their product lines, delivery modes, turnaround times and in-stock positions? How does their service stack up to yours? Taking the time to train all staff on this kind of information will pay off. Also, teach them where to obtain this information and encourage them to keep up with changes on an ongoing basis.
3. Finally, help your employees get the big picture of what's going on in your industry. This can be accomplished through regular lunch-and-learns for all staff. Keep all staff in the loop about what's been learned at trade shows, industry associations and other sources.

Curious frontline staff can learn much from customers and other salespeople. Ensure that all staff are encouraged to collect and distribute any feedback information to appropriate people throughout the company.

One word of caution: Obsess over customers, not the competition. While it is important to know what the competition is doing, too much examination can distract you from your goal of building your own loyal relationships. The most important information you have on your products and services is between your customers' ears—and how they apply it to their world to make their lives easier.

12. TRAIN ON INTERNAL SYSTEMS AND PARTNERS

Aside from products, customer-care providers need to understand how internal systems at their own company work. They need to see the big picture and their role in it. How does the workflow happen; what is the paper trail required; how does accounting get and provide information? Understand that people are not computers, which can download quantities of information quickly and recall just as quickly. People need to hear a new piece of information several times—technical information often as many as six times—to embed it in their long-term memory. Ensure new employees have a variety of learning opportunities, from job shadowing to discussions over lunch with key people, to handbooks and manuals. Remember, there are a variety of learning methods and people have preferences.

One way to give new frontline employees the big picture is

to have them temporarily work in different departments. Certainly customer-care employees should understand the departments with which they will be working closely, such as sales, the warehouse, shipping/receiving and accounting. Pairing them with a positive, knowledgeable employee is key. Those "teaching" employees should be briefed on what to cover. Remind them that their time spent together is also about building a relationship with the new employee. The new employee is someone with whom they will be interacting, so creating rapport is important for both.

Human Resources can have a role to play in onboarding a new customer-care provider, but not every company has a full-time, or even a part-time, human resources manager. Smaller companies need to involve the direct supervisor, the general manager or the owner in this process.

Onboarding a new customer-care employee should focus on both the cultural aspects and the technical needs of the new hire. Cultural aspects of the role must be delivered internally, but if technical assistance is required, it can be outsourced. Getting up to speed and becoming productive quickly is important, but it's most successful when employees can look back on the experience and tell you how helpful it was.

Finally, preparation is key. Having checklists of tasks for onboarding will ensure nothing falls through the cracks and all employees have a consistent, positive experience. Getting present employees' input into the process will enrich the experience.

Ask questions like: "What would have helped you in the first 30/60/90 days on the job?" You'll get answers from the experts.

13. SET CLEAR CUSTOMER-SERVICE EXPECTATIONS

Training on customer-service-level expectations should be clear, written, concise and reinforced. It's not fair to get upset with employees for doing things you didn't tell them they shouldn't do! In other words, most employers hire people and expect them to use their "common sense" in customer service. But not everyone has the same background in this regard. Specifics around expectations need to be spelled out for them. Without specific guidance, they will do what makes sense to them, but not necessarily to you. This often results in an expectation gap in behaviors and eventual conflict.

Manners are rarely mentioned in onboarding processes for any employees. If the expectations are that an employee will dress or behave in a certain way, these should be spelled out. In one company where I worked, there was an expectation that guests were walked to the elevator after a meeting. In another, guests were walked to the front door and a cab was hailed for them. Expectations vary.

When I started my own company, I didn't institute a dress code. I quickly found that was a mistake. I regretted not starting it from the beginning. I could have avoided some pushback and line-crossing if the code had been a condition of employment. Employees don't mind guidelines as long as they are fair, equitable and well-communicated.

Training on phone and email etiquette is also becoming more

and more important in an electronic world where these tools are so commonplace. Guidelines on how customers will be treated over communication lines should include telephone etiquette and the rules of the company.

Standards of moral and ethical behavior in the company can be spelled out as long as they don't infringe on human rights. It is only fair to describe the culture of accountability if there is one, including what the employee should expect to be accountable for daily, weekly and monthly. Expectations around collaboration and working with others should be included in this training. Finally, there should be very clear guidelines around decision making. Delineate what the employee can decide on his own and what should be escalated to a supervisor.

CHAPTER 4

Second Level Training

14. TRAIN FOR BASIC COMMUNICATION

Let's face it, frontline employees are communicators. Whether by phone, email or online, it's what they do all day, every day. Every relationship they build is simply a series of conversations. The quality of their communication dictates the nature of their relationships.

Conversations, therefore, can be relationship-building or relationship-killing. Some of the key ingredients of conversations are the words you choose, your tonality and your body language. An awareness of how one sounds to others is the beginning of empathy and good manners.

Body Language

Strangely enough, body language is the strongest form of communication. You can tell more about people's attitude toward you through body language than through anything else—and so can they about you. From eye contact to posture to facial expressions, you telegraph your message to customers instantly through body language. If customer-care providers roll their eyes, what does that say? The message is likely that they don't care, without a word being spoken. However, if their expression is one of pure empathy, the message is, "I completely understand; how can I help you?" Often people are not aware of the messages they're sending.

Tonality

Sarcasm, ridicule and disinterest can drip from a person's tonality and often send unspoken messages. Many medical malpractice lawsuits are a result of a condescending tonality rather than the actual medical mistake. People want to feel good about themselves, and if they do not, they will seek acceptance elsewhere—like your competition.

Spoken Word

Communication training is key for customer-care providers since the essence of their role is to be a professional communicator. Customer-care providers need to learn to choose their words wisely since they will stay with the customer for a long time. To paraphrase Maya Angelou, your customers may not remember your exact words, but they'll remember how you made them feel.

How people communicate depends on their style and behavior preferences, along with their personality. Personalities are difficult to understand sometimes, but behavioral preferences often are patterns and can be recognized, either by natural instinct or, more often, by communication training. Raise the communication awareness of your customer-care professionals, and you'll create better communicators with better relationships.

No Mutual Mystification

If you've ever walked away or hung up from a customer unsure about what happens next, then you understand what mutual mystification is. It is an incomplete understanding of who is meant to do what next.

Customers can sometimes have "happy ears." You say, "We'll try to deliver on Thursday," and they hear, "We will deliver on Thursday." Make it a practice to recap the conversation after interactions with customers, confirming exactly what has been said and what happens next. Make sure you understand what their expectations are. Now is the time to manage them, not when disappointment sets in at delivery time.

It might be helpful to ask: "Does anyone have anything to add? Did I miss anything or misunderstand anything?" Eliminating mutual mystification today reduces the opportunity for misunderstandings and unfulfilled expectations tomorrow.

Summary of Basic Communication

Train communication techniques that build awareness of how words, tonality and body language impact the customer, such as communication techniques that help employees read others and situations quickly and accurately. Train techniques that result in better reactions from frontline employees, and you will provide better outcomes for customers.

15. TRAIN FOR QUESTIONING AND LISTENING

Remember the childhood game of whispering a phrase to someone and asking them to pass it on? By the time it reached the fourth or fifth person, the meaning of the original phrase was lost! Then, it amused us; in customer care, it can be costly. Teaching questioning and listening skills will help managers, customers, internal customers and the employees themselves.

Are you a good listener? Most people would answer "yes" to this question. After all, they believe they hear everything that is said to them. In reality, though, there is much more to it. Mastering the skill of listening has many roadblocks that must be removed first.

The first roadblock is a belief that you already know or understand the situation. In customer care, the same issues are often heard repeatedly. Before the customer is through his first sentence, customer-care providers have jumped to conclusions about the issue and the fix.

Another roadblock is a defensive stance. Customer-care

Second Level Training

providers want to argue and defend rather than empathetically listen to the customer. Another manifestation of defensiveness is being competitive and only listening until a break, when providers can jump in and satisfy their own egos by showing how smart they are.

Finally, a roadblock is being passive. It's not enough to listen to your customers—you must prove that you listen. You do that with active listening skills: confirming questions, eye contact, body language and tonality. Listening is often referred to as the "highest form of respect" (according to author Tom Peters).

When a customer is seeking help or is upset, he needs to vent his issue uninterrupted. Jumping in with a solution too soon can cause further frustration. Don't prejudge. Allow people to explain their needs and then ask clarifying questions. You may think you know what they need, but unless you allow them to explain, you can get it wrong and waste time.

Listening is an activity done with all forms of communication—silence, tonality, spoken words and body language. It's done with a laser focus on more than hearing—it's done for meaning and understanding. Sometimes it's what's not being said that is most important. Often the intent is missed because of a personal agenda or because a reply is being formulated without listening.

So, once again, are you a good listener? Or do you recognize that some work may need to be done in this area? Train to an awareness of listening shortcomings and respectful listening skills.

Developing good questioning skills is also key. Who asks great questions? You might think of lawyers, doctors, teachers—all professionals actually. How about airline pilots? They have to exchange the same piece of information and have it confirmed up to six times with co-pilots or the control tower before executing directions. They have to know how to ask the right question and listen to the answer with attention. Lives depend upon it.

Anyone who needs to get to the bottom of an issue must be proficient at constructing and asking compelling questions. Frontline service providers are similar to the professionals above in that they must diagnose problems and prescribe a fix. The better they are at getting to the root of the problem, the more productive they can be. Questioning is the most proactive productivity tool imaginable.

One way customer-care providers get themselves in trouble is by rushing to answer a customer's question before they uncover the intent that's driving the question. The question you hear is probably not the real question. The intent behind that question is far more important than the surface meaning of the words. Here's an example:

> A furnace oil delivery company would get a flurry of calls the first cold day of the fall, all asking the same question: "How much is your oil per gallon today?" The customer-service representatives would quickly give people the answer.
>
> Instead, as trainers, we got them to respond this way: "Certainly, let me look that up for you. While I do, can I

ask you a question? What made you pick up the phone and call us today?"

The answers they received shocked the reps. Over 60 percent of the callers' primary reasons were not related to low price, but to service breakdowns with their present suppliers. Answers like letting their tanks run dry, persistent billing problems and no local technicians were very common. They were all issues where our client could beat the competition.

Once the customer-service frontline staff learned not to answer the "how much" question so quickly, they were able to engage in service conversations that brought many new customers to the company.

Rather than answer the question, try reversing it back to the customer to uncover the underlying intent. Some reversing questions include:

- "Why do you ask?"
- "What made you reach out to us today?"
- "What were you hoping to hear?"
- "May I ask why that's important to you?"

Having a toolbox filled with questioning techniques gives frontline service providers the methodology to dig into the underlying causes of a problem unobtrusively while still maintaining, or even building, a relationship with the customer.

One of the most important questions asked is permission:

permission to ask a question, permission to put on hold, permission to look into the issue. "Is it OK if I ask you some questions to understand what's happened to date?" This question gives the customer a sense of control while actually handing control of the conversation over to the service provider.

Good questions can build strong relationships. They help you focus on your customer and guide him through a great customer-care or sales experience. Bad questions can drip with condescension—"So, did you plug it in?"—and make a customer feel not-OK about himself and negative about you. Scan any website that reports poor customer-care experiences, and you will see dozens of questions riddled with sarcasm, ridicule and condescension.

Mastery of questioning techniques puts the customer first and ensures that he has a good experience.

16. TRAIN FOR DEALING WITH DIFFICULT PEOPLE

Having a process is a wonderful benefit. Imagine baking a cake without a recipe or filling in an accounting spreadsheet without formulas. Processes give you step-by-step methods with predictable outcomes. Now imagine you are a customer-service provider fielding calls or visits daily from frustrated, angry, worried, concerned or emotional customers. What might eventually happen to you without a process to keep you on track? Might you become exhausted? Might you look to change careers?

Training employees on a process to handle difficult people

and situations removes stress, calms the situation and moves a customer from emotional to calm in the most productive way possible. This process must be carefully constructed to ensure customers can vent their frustrations fully, feel as though they're being heard, answer questions when they feel they are ready and allow the customer-care provider to move to solving their problem at the right pace.

For the customer-service provider's part, he must be able to read the signals, question empathetically and be an Olympic listener. This requires a high level of communication training and practice. The results can be palpable for the service provider as his confidence, his ability to handle challenging situations and his value to the company grows.

If you don't train your people in these delicate skills, it can lead to lost sales, lost customers and burned-out employees. If those burned-out employees leave, that is one kind of loss. If they stay and continue in their positions, that's another.

One of the greatest supports you can give your employees, with the greatest return on investment, is teaching them a process to deal with difficult people and challenging situations. When you're having a difficult conversation, it's easy to either get wrapped up in your own emotions and needs or get hooked into the customer's frustration or emotions. Unfortunately, that doesn't help reach a resolution. Seeing things from the customer's point of view and asking what you can do to move toward resolution is a start. Once customers recognize your empathy and desire for resolution, you're moving toward fixing the first problem—their emotional state. Then you can move toward fixing the issue, whatever it is. Meeting their needs will meet your needs.

It's Just Business; Don't Take It Personally

The best inoculation you can give your frontline workers is a resistance to criticism, ridicule, sarcasm, condescension and outright negativity. Whether dealing with the public or in a business-to-business setting, they will experience these regularly. Some people want what they want and will say anything to get it. Handling these situations starts with a deep belief that, whether you've made the mistake or not, this is about resolution, not about you personally.

Understanding conversational interactions through tools like transactional analysis helps to pinpoint the difference between productive and unproductive conversations. It also helps to understand what kind of conversations fuel difficult situations and which can diffuse them.

Don't send your customer-service providers into a conflict without the tools they need to resolve it and the protection they need to survive it.

Deconstructing Transactions

For years I owned a small chain of children's stores with a partner. We sold children's books and imaginative toys, and our stores were filled with moms, dads and children. Sounds like a fun place to work, doesn't it? But for our staff, it was stressful.

We were often witness to temper tantrums, unsupervised children, family arguments, stressed grandmothers and every form of family conflict you can imagine. It gave amazing insight into human behavior. But it wasn't until I was immersed in Sandler with its core of transactional analysis that I began to understand the source of interpersonal conflict and how to protect myself and my customer-service providers from stress and burnout.

Sandler uses transactional analysis—a close examination of the conversations people have—to understand the dance that happens between buyer and seller. I immediately made the same connection in a customer-care setting. Most customer-care providers are hired because they love to help; however, they avoid conflict as much as possible. I found that if they were aware of the typical interactions that go on within conversations, they were better able to not only avoid conflict, but to stop it in its tracks when it did occur.

CHAPTER 5

Senior Level Training

17. TRAIN FOR READING PEOPLE

The understanding of customers can be enhanced with training in DISC, transactional analysis and the OK/Not-OK principle.

Most soft skills begin with an awareness of self. One example of this is using the DISC communications model to understand your own preferred style and how divergent it is from that of another person. DISC first differentiates between task orientation and people orientation in preferences. Many customer-care providers are a combination of the two, easily working with people but also being able to organize and accomplish many tasks daily. On the other hand, they come to recognize that those who are not people-oriented but are highly task-oriented may, to the customer-care provider, appear tough, demanding and unfeeling.

Next, DISC differentiates between active and expressive versus reserved and thoughtful behavior. Those who are active will often tell you exactly what they want without prompting, while the reserved may be more indirect communicators and need much more information. These two vectors (people/task and active/reserved) give the axis-based DISC profile that describes four behavioral preferences.

Imagine a CEO calling into your customer-care department with a list of demands and deadlines, gruffly barking orders and abruptly hanging up. When your frontline staff understands that this person is highly task-oriented and prefers a very direct communication style, it makes it easier both to respond and not take what was said personally. In other words, they are able to read the customer better and manage their own reactions better.

Similarly, transactional analysis training is a tool that customer-care providers find useful. Transactional analysis (TA) is a framework for describing behavior in an interchange between two people. It helps customer-care providers to understand why prospects and customers react the way they do, particularly when selling or dealing with a problem. It's an analytical thinking process that provides insight and gives frontline employees control over their actions and reactions.

The power embedded in this tool to "read" or understand where a customer is coming from is invaluable. Based on the three ego states of Parent, Adult and Child, TA describes various conversational interchanges that are useful and productive and those that are repetitive and damaging. It places the power for creating productive interchanges squarely with the customer-care provider.

Both DISC and TA training are powerful tools if they become part of the culture of your company and a language is created around their use. This happens when everyone has the same knowledge of these tools and they become part of the company vernacular. Because customer-care providers and salespeople are on the front lines of communication with your customer base daily, they are the ideal people to become professional communicators. Every tool you can put in their toolbox to accomplish this is valuable.

Reinforcing these tools is accomplished through role-playing and daily application. Make it a part of your company's world.

18. TRAIN FOR FINDING SALES OPPORTUNITIES

When asked who in the company is responsible for sales, most owners would answer, "Everyone." However, depending on the role, there will be different expectations of employees. Customer-service providers are well-positioned to maintain and grow present business through excellent service and strong relationships. This doesn't preclude them from probing for more business opportunities. But if they have not done this in the past, they may have a reluctance or a preconceived notion of what sales is. They likely don't have a process in place that will give them the comfort level they need to try any kind of sales questioning.

Many people earned money selling lemonade in their driveway as children. They remember how much fun that was, yet when asked to sell in the customer-care role, they will resist. Generally it's because they don't feel prepared for the role. They haven't been trained on a process to follow.

Opportunity Finding

> While filling a homeowner's oil tank one frosty morning in January, Justin noticed a moving truck next door. His customer noticed him watching and reported: "The Fergusons have moved out. You might want to check with the new owners. I know the Fergusons heated with oil."
>
> Justin didn't see a car around and figured there was no use talking to moving men so he did nothing. Back at the office later that day, it completely slipped his mind, so he didn't mention it to the inside sales team. In the end, the new neighbors were soon approached by Justin's competition and won the business. Justin missed an opportunity. The biggest part of sales is showing up.
>
> What if Justin had asked his clients a few more questions? "You wouldn't know the names of the new owners, would you? Any chance I could call you on Monday when they arrive and get that information from you? I think I'll just slip a business card in the door right now." There was a

number of behaviors that would have put Justin at the front of that line, but they didn't happen.

Often customer-care providers, technical support people and other employees are reluctant to engage in any kind of sales conversation. Worse, they may have the attitude of, "That's not my job." I'm quite sure the technician in question had that attitude. I'm also sure the owner of his company would disagree. Opportunities for business are everywhere, and training an awareness for finding those opportunities is the first step in expanding your sales force and creating a well-oiled, systematic way of finding new opportunities.

Don't be frustrated with employees who don't recognize sales opportunities. This is something that must be trained. It's an attitude, a technique and an ongoing behavior that will create a return on investment for you for years to come.

Prospecting Attitude

If your customer-care providers are tasked with outbound calls, you will need to give them: 1) a proven process for making those calls, 2) clear expectations around the desired results and 3) a schedule and accountability process. Becoming more productive around sales can bolster employee confidence and competence.

The "Qualifying" Approach to Sales

Understanding that sales is not about presenting but about qualifying is the next attitude shift that customer-care providers need. "Qualifying" simply means figuring out whether customers are a good match for your products and services. They have a problem that your products/services can solve; they can afford to buy that solution; they can make the decision to purchase in a timely manner. Arming customer-care providers with the right questions, next steps and a process can give them a greater comfort level with asking the qualifying questions.

If you don't challenge customer-care providers' belief systems around selling and provide the guidance to be successful, you will need to challenge your own expectations around outcomes. Contrary to popular belief, salespeople are not born. They may have some qualities that make selling easier, but training all employees (whether in a key sales role or not) in the importance of sales and opportunity finding is key. In this way, company expectations are satisfied and both the sales force and top-line revenues will continue to grow.

19. TRAIN ASSERTIVENESS, NOT AGGRESSIVENESS

For many, customer service is their first job in the workplace. Many have not yet developed the confidence to establish and maintain boundaries with customers and coworkers. Sometimes assertiveness is confused with aggressiveness or confrontation, and they are reluctant to speak up. This can be frustrating to employees, customers and managers. Being able to set boundaries is important with external customers, but also with internal customers—coworkers, vendors, managers. Being able to say "no" and expressing dissatisfaction or disagreement is part of everyone's job. Doing it well so as not to inflame issues is a learned behavior.

Understanding what assertiveness means, the intent behind it and the proper way to express it will raise the comfort level of customer-service providers. If assertiveness is done with respect for self and for others, it should never be confrontational or aggressive. Understanding that you can keep relationships intact even when you have to agree to disagree is critical. Assertiveness simply means standing up for self when others cross the line and doing it such that you are taken seriously while not distancing others.

Shouldn't part of any training in customer service be a discussion on where the line should be drawn with abusive, inappropriate or pushy customers?

Jonathan had been on the job in the call center for six months. His supervisor Amanda was a great support to him, guiding him along and encouraging him to see mistakes as part of the learning process. But there was one kind of customer that Jonathan dreaded. Customers who were pushy and overly demanding always left him feeling drained. When it came right down to it, Jonathan believed that customers were always right. He shied away from saying "no" and bent over backwards to provide whatever was requested, even when it meant the company would lose money. Needless to say this often put in Jonathan in conflict with Amanda.

"Just tell him what you can do and draw the line there," explained Amanda in a case where a customer was demanding a full refund for a product that was more than two years old. It was guaranteed for only one year.

"But he won't accept that from me," replied Jonathan.

"No," replied Amanda, "you won't accept that from you. Jonathan, this is about your own boundaries, not the company's or the customer's. It's time you started asserting the company's and your rights. Let's discuss how you can do that."

For some employees, assertiveness can take years to develop. For others, it doesn't develop at all. But assertiveness is something that can be trained, coached and mentored. After years of training both salespeople and customer-care professionals, I find that an understanding of assertiveness can result in some pulling back on their aggressiveness and others developing a calming assertiveness that builds confidence.

When my youngest daughter was in primary school, she came home crying one day. She explained that every day on the snowy school ground, one of the boys in her class would grab her hat and not give it back. She would cry, create a scene and eventually tell the teacher, who would intervene to retrieve her hat.

I asked her if she'd like to learn a good line that would get her hat back without getting into conflict with the boy. "Yes!" she said.

"OK, the next time he takes your hat here's what you say to him: 'When you're done with my hat, I want it back.' Then calmly walk away." I explained what "tone of voice" meant and had her practice the line. "Don't be mad; don't yell at him. Just be calm."

"You think that will work?" she asked.

"Try it and see!"

The next day she practically flew off the bus to me. "It worked! It worked! I got my hat back. I didn't even need the teacher's help!"

What my daughter had learned was to diffuse the emotion of the situation by calmly and assertively knowing what to say. The little boy wanted a "show." When the button he pushed didn't work, he lost his power position and became disinterested. This can be applied to customer-service situations as well. When you calmly yet assertively explain to the customer what you can do, what the next steps are and the lengths to which you can go, it creates the boundaries necessary to protect the company. Naturally, some customers will always push beyond established limits, but the more good responses and assertiveness training your frontline caregivers have, the more confidence they will have to handle anything thrown at them.

CHAPTER 6

Ongoing Reinforcement Training

20. CONTINUE TO TRAIN ADVANCED COMMUNICATION SKILLS

After driving safely for over 20 years, I was stopped for speeding. Rather than lose points on my license, I elected to take the written test again and avoid increased insurance rates. My husband brought home the driver handbook, which I ignored. I had already passed the test at 16, and I had 20 years of experience on top of that! Why would I need to learn anything new?

I learned the answer as I read the exam questions. My heart sank as I realized what I had forgotten or never knew. I failed the exam by one point. Only after a good "talking to" by the adjudicator was I handed the two points and allowed to leave. Lesson learned. What I had was 20 years to forget what I originally knew and to develop bad habits.

The most dangerous of learners are the ones who believe they already know everything. The second most dangerous are those who hear something and say, "I already knew that." Knowing is not the same as being able to do.

It would be ideal if you could train employees once and they would change attitudes, learn new techniques and have good habits permanently. Typically this is not the case, as the story above illustrates. Over time people can slip back into old ways and bad habits. In the familiarity and busyness of day-to-day work, standards can slip. A refresher, update or tune-up is due when you begin to notice signs.

The first sign is revealed in the vocabulary staff uses in customer care. The language of customer care is the language of calming, apology/questioning and active listening. When you hear terse brick-wall language, condescending tonality or frustration levels in your frontline service providers, it may be time to train communications again.

The next sign is a rise in attrition rates without an obvious explanation. Customers may be leaving due to inattention or unaddressed complaints. Whatever is happening, an injection of training and renewed adherence to standards may be needed.

When you notice that internal conflict is more prevalent, it could be a sign that frontline people need a shot of empathy training. Employees often become jaded from hearing the same internal customer issues repeatedly, and this can lead to an overall frustration level. A well-oiled internal process is built on a high standard of communication. Anything less and breakdowns lead to continued conflict and a toxic workplace.

An ongoing learning path keeps employees engaged. It renews their commitment to the company, to customers and to each other. It can make them feel valued and respected. A disengaged employee is an employee with one foot out the door.

Whether it is through formal training, ongoing coaching or formal or informal mentoring, all employees want to feel part of company culture and that they are valued contributors to company growth. Long-term commitment to the continued professional and personal growth of your most strategic, customer-facing employees can accomplish this.

CHAPTER 7

Sandler Rules for Process

Customer service is not a department. It is a chain of activities throughout the company aimed at helping customers get what they want easily and quickly. A smooth process allows for time savings for the customers and for you. Good processes can minimize the number of touches required by the customers and therefore reduce the chance of problems. Process allows for a seamless combination of customer choice between live-person interaction and technology-based service. Finally, good processes can give customers an overall easier experience with better outcomes.

Here are the rules for good processes:

21. Create service processes based on what customers really want.

22. Keep your processes simple.
23. Have a management process.
24. Have a process for failure.
25. Build flexibility into every process.
26. Process the detailed grunt work.
27. Have a process for problem resolution.
28. Have a process to win back ghosts.
29. Have a process for continuous improvement.

People have systems for everything—taking a shower, landing a plane, accounting, even how to drive home from the office each evening. Systems are critical in customer care, and the smoother the system, the happier the customer.

The way your customer experiences your company is dictated by both your people and your process. Does your system make it easy for your customers to do business with you?

The order is written, and the customer-service representative enters it into the database, which produces paperwork for the warehouse, which fills the order and passes it on to shipping. Shipping sends it off for delivery, and the representative receives notice back that it has been delivered. The representative then touches base with the new customer to ensure everything was as expected and to thank him for the business. Everyone who touched that order is in the customer-care business. The systems that flow through the company should be geared toward serving the customer, not the system.

21. CREATE SERVICE PROCESSES BASED ON WHAT CUSTOMERS REALLY WANT

Customer service is like a toothbrush—you can't borrow mine. Companies have different markets, customer bases, product and service offerings and cultures. Although you can cherry-pick other companies' good behaviors, creating your own customer-service culture is a result of knowing and communicating with your customers. Are you customer-driven? Do you understand what your customers want and value? It's easy to think you know, but if you haven't taken the time to ask them, you might have more to learn.

Also, how well do you deliver what customers want? Most customers want working with you to be the following (in no particular order):

Easy

Customers want you to make it easy for them—easy to understand the products and services, easy to acquire them and easy to use them.

Quick

This is the age of "instant"—electronic passes in your car so you don't have to slow down at toll booths, high-speed Internet and remote controls for everything, etc. Customers don't want to wait for satisfaction; they want it now.

Accurate

Customers want you to deliver it right the first time. They

don't want to open their order and find that they've been sent the wrong size and have to return it. However, customers understand that mistakes happen. At these times, they want you to make it right—quickly and easily.

Good Value

It used to be that customers wanted it cheap—cheaper than everyone else. However, sophisticated buyers understand that a cheap purchase price doesn't always deliver the value they're seeking. An inexpensive printer may have very expensive ink cartridges that in the long run will cost more. Customers want value, and that value may be in the form of the salespeople, the ease of working with you or another "value add."

What Is Value?

A manager recently told me, "I'm not 100 percent sure what our value proposition is. How can my people work on it, if it's not defined? I know we're not the cheapest, and we're geographically farther away."

A short conversation revealed that none of his competition had the wealth of up-to-date product knowledge that his team had. Nor did the competition reach out to connect their clients with new products and services that could enhance their jobs or productivity. His competitors couldn't match this manager's turnaround times nor the levels of personal service his team provided.

By the end of the conversation we had identified five key values his team exemplified: trustworthiness, credibility, personal relationships, being an information resource and providing a connection to the best products or services for the customer's needs. In truth, value like this will trump price and geography every time.

Personal

Customers want personal service. They want you to know their name, to tailor your products to their needs—almost know what they want before they ask for it. They want to feel special and important.

22. KEEP YOUR PROCESSES SIMPLE

Given a choice of taking the stairs or an elevator, many would choose the elevator. It's quicker, it takes less effort and it gets you to the same place. In the role of customer, the same rule applies. The easier it is to do business with a company, the more likely the customer will repeat. Why do some companies understand this and some don't?

Matt's boss asked him to procure shelving for a warehouse expansion that was nearing completion. He called three companies and explained exactly what was needed, the timeline and the general budget. All three seemed anxious to work with him and promised him information.

One salesperson called back later that day and told him that he would need to fill out a credit application before he could deliver a quote. Matt agreed to complete the form and faxed it back within a few hours. The promised day for the quote to arrive came and went, and Matt had still not received a quote from that company. When he called the salesperson, he was told: "We're still waiting to hear back from your financial references."

"We may not even buy from you, and you're bothering our credit references?" Matt was furious. "Tell you what, send them a note and tell them not to bother. We'll find our shelving somewhere else."

All things being equal, if the process a customer must go through to do business with you is too complicated, the customer will default to an easier option.

Successful customer-focused companies have a step-by-step approach and streamline and adjust their system for customer ease of use. They don't just do one big thing right. They do dozens of little things right. They have clearly defined processes for returns and restocking, for new account setup, for shipping and for incoming and outbound customer-care calls.

In some companies, a process will arise out of necessity. Customers may be failing to pay in the required 30 days, so the company institutes a much stricter new-account-setup policy. Now new clients must give three credit references and keep a credit card on file, and salespeople won't earn commission on payments later than 60 days. But the problem may not have been the customers. Maybe it is a high error rate on invoices or an employee in collections is not suited to that position. Rather than address the actual problem, the company has increased the burden on the customer and made it more difficult for him to do business. This is just one example where a burdensome internal process can negatively impact customer relationships.

What small things can you easily change? Ask customers: "What is one thing we can do better to make your experience with us more beneficial to you?" Ask employees: "What is one thing we could do better or differently that would make a difference in your interactions with customers?" Then, of course, listen to and act on that feedback. It's only a baby step, but it is a great place to start. To quote Neil Armstrong, "That's one small step for man, one giant leap for mankind."

A culture of constant improvement is not about perfection, it's about the process of making mistakes, learning from them and improving. Don't hang back waiting for the one big thing that will improve customer service. Improve it in repeatable, small steps. Small steps are easier—easier to get going in the first place and easier to make into a sustainable process.

Each time a new step is taken, it must be sustainable. Remember to train, review and retrain the basics over and over again. Despite what most believe, no one retains everything they learn and often people slip back into old habits. Never assume that frontline people are adhering to processes. Check in and support them with each change over time, and don't allow people to sink back into their "elevator" comfort zones. Put the energy and effort into taking the stairs and become stronger over time.

23. HAVE A MANAGEMENT PROCESS

When you hire good frontline staff, ensure you are training supervisors and managers in the systems they'll need to enforce daily. Too often good people are lost to supervisors who don't have a management system, a customer-service vision or great communication skills.

Just because you are a good customer-care provider or trainer doesn't mean you will make a good manager or leader. It is a different skill set. It depends on a set of behaviors, not a set of rules.

- **Behavior #1:** Don't manage from behind your desk. Get out, mingle, talk to employees, talk to customers. Let them see your management in action.
- **Behavior #2:** Ask for feedback and write it down immediately; let the employee or the customer see you writing it down. Take feedback seriously and act on it for constant improvement.
- **Behavior #3:** Do what your customer-care people do. Regularly sit in their chairs, take the calls and deal with customers so you can relate to your employees with real-world examples. If you are seen to be an "ivory tower manager," you may lose credibility and respect.
- **Behavior #4:** Innovate and institute change—not for change's sake, but to improve customer care, relationships and the work lives of your employees.
- **Behavior #5:** Regularly catch your people doing things

right. Encouragement is a huge motivator and is a great way to build morale and a loyal workforce.

- **Behavior #6:** Understand that customer-service providers will treat customers the way they are treated. Employees follow the behavior patterns of their supervisors; employees are actually customers of their supervisors and should be treated that way. Use friendly greetings, respect, flexibility in accommodating requests, listening and questioning—all the things that you expect your people to do with customers, you should do with them. Modeled behavior is more powerful than "do as I say."

Owners, managers and supervisors often underestimate the issue of employee affiliation. They blame frontline employees for being "difficult" or "resistant to change." They are reluctant to introduce changes because of the perceived pushback that may occur. But customer-care providers want to do a good job for customers. They want to be part of an organization that puts customer satisfaction first.

Customer-care management can be broken down into four roles—supervising, coaching, training and mentoring. Each role is important and comes with its challenges. Problems arise when one of these roles begins to take the lion's share of a manager's time. Typically, that is supervising. Management that relies heavily on supervising includes plenty of firefighting—solving problems for employees that they should know how to solve themselves. Management that relies heavily on coaching often means that the managers are enabling their people to repeatedly rely on them for answers. Management that too heavily relies on training can result in employees not taking on personal responsibility to implement and self-direct. Management that heavily relies on mentoring may result in spotty results—very good for some employees and no results at all for others.

Obviously, supervision is important. You always need to know what is going on with your employees. You need to "detect and correct" when you see poor communication skills and bad customer-service habits. It's a great way to discover where training and/or coaching is needed. The first time an employee brings you a problem, it may be a training opportunity. On the other hand, if that employee is bringing you the same issue over and over again, it is time for some coaching to find out what's behind the inability to move ahead on his own. Perhaps it is a confidence issue or he has not understood the process for fixing the issue. It's a one-on-one opportunity to uncover a problem and to solve it once and for all.

Managers need to lend weight to training by being involved themselves, by ensuring each employee's training path is suitable and effective, by establishing required behavioral outcomes and by holding employees accountable for those outcomes. Too often when training is announced, frontline employees roll their eyes and ask what the "flavor of the month" is now. This is a result of management not finding a system that works and sticking to that system.

Training can come from inside or outside the company. But beware of cross training—when you arrange for a veteran salesperson to spend time on the job with a new hire. It's an effective tool if the trainees are gaining insight and hindsight. However, you may also find that the veterans pass along poor attitudes and habits if paired with the wrong person. Don't depend on your present employees to fully train and onboard new employees. That's a much bigger job.

To address self-confidence, self-direction and self-esteem issues, mentoring may be the answer. It can also bridge the gap from a prior job's culture to your own company's for new members of the team. Not all employees are open to the concept, but for those who have a thirst for development and enjoy challenges, mentorship can have excellent outcomes both for the employees' career path and the company's culture. For more established employees, it can groom them for new expanded roles within the company and establish a career path that keeps them engaged and motivated.

The manager's role is to ensure employee success. Even if training is outsourced, it must be reinforced by the manager through coaching and mentorship. Tools like debriefing, planning, setting goals, performance evaluation and reinforcement are key. Otherwise, the training has no stickiness and the company has wasted time, money and energy that could have been more effectively invested.

24. HAVE A PROCESS FOR FAILURE

Every company has them. Call them failures, customer-service breakdowns or change opportunities, they're guaranteed to happen occasionally. Unless you have a process established that creates a learning path from these occurrences, they may be doomed to be repeated.

A learning path toward minimizing failures may look like this:

1. Ask those who experienced or observed the breakdown to report exactly what happened. Ensure it's a safe environment where personal responsibility is taken and participants are kept safe. This is not an excuse to reprimand—it's a learning opportunity.
2. Bring the issue to a larger group and brainstorm by asking the "one" question: "What is the one thing that we might have said, asked or done differently that might have resulted in a better outcome in this situation?"
3. Ask your frontline people to come up with a rule of thumb or process that would either avoid the situation in the future or better resolve it when it does occur. Emphasize that the process gives them step-by-step actions toward a logical outcome, but that they can always use their own common sense when dealing with customers.
4. Finally, ensure that everyone is aware of the issue, the discussion, the resolution path and the outcomes.

Customer-service providers need to understand there is no shame in having failed occasionally. There is, however, a problem with not recognizing failures, trying to sweep them under the rug or not learning from them to create a better way forward in the future.

For some, failure can be an end—a place to get stuck in a downward spiral of self-recrimination and doubt. Failure is not an excuse for discouragement, self-pity, blame or retribution. Failure is an opportunity to move another step toward success. Linger on failure only long enough to get your lesson learned and develop new strategies, tactics and winning behaviors. Use failure as a vehicle to look forward to the future and couple it with the question: "What are we going to do about it?" If management and supervisors have this attitude, it will spread throughout the company.

Above all, failure should not be taken personally. It is a group failure, not a personal failure, and it's an opportunity for the group. Risks should not be discouraged and punished. If employees only learn to do what's always been done, there will be no room for improvement. Even though failure happens to one person, it is likely something that could happen to anyone under similar circumstances. Most successful people will tell you they don't dwell on failure. They visualize themselves being more successful next time, and they move on. Most successful companies do the same.

As part of learning, look at your customers as a community. When you engage them in the conversation of improvement, listen to their ideas and act on their suggestions. Technology has a large role to play in this feedback, but directly asking customers that same "one" question is key: "If there were one thing we could have done better or differently to make your experience with our company better, what would that be?"

There is no shame in admitting you are involved in a constant improvement process. Your customers are the most valuable feedback vehicle you have—and a key part of that process.

25. BUILD FLEXIBILITY INTO EVERY PROCESS

It's been said many times: Hire good people, train them to serve customers, manage their expectations, reward them properly, show them the goalposts and let them fulfill their mandate. Regulations differ from systems in that they are hard policies, whereas systems are the step-by-step techniques used to achieve a desired outcome.

When you overregulate in an attempt to standardize the customer-service experience, you often take the human element out of engagement with customers. Worse, you train your people to say things like: "We're not allowed to do that," "We can't adjust that for you," or, "Sorry, that's not our policy." There is no bigger red flag to a customer than to hear this kind of explanation. There is, of course, a certain risk in allowing frontline people to make decisions on the spot. Sometimes they may give away too much; sometimes they may make the wrong decision. But there is risk in not allowing them decision-making power as well. They may become disengaged if they feel they have no power to do their job—that is, to create a satisfied customer. Frontline service providers should receive model behavior to follow. A new employee need only look around to see great decision making in action. Customer-service decision making is a learned behavior.

It can be learned by observing a good supervisor/manager. It can be learned by seeing it in action with well-trained coworkers.

Employees in general learn the outcomes of making mistakes in a company. If you make a decision that turns out to be wrong and are shamed for it, you learn to rely on rigid policies. If you make a mistake and are praised for making a decision, together with having received good training on the goalposts, you will grow in confidence and make good decisions more and more often.

The culture that managers create in relation to regulations can be one of three kinds:

- First: Do what I say; follow the rules.
- Second: Think for yourself, but listen to me.
- Third: Creatively think for yourself and learn from each situation.

Which culture do you think would be best for your customers and your customer-service providers? Self-regulation is the ability to stay calmly focused and controlled. The more customer-care providers achieve self-regulation, the more they can communicate and provide solutions. Self-regulation is not about simply complying with company rules. It's about growing in confidence and competence because you've developed an ability to cope with difficult situations and manage your own fears and negative emotions.

Every employee has guidelines or rules to which he must adhere. Try not to put rules in place that are so cumbersome or unfair that employees will find themselves constantly on the defensive.

26. PROCESS THE DETAILED GRUNT WORK

Not all customer care is face-to-face, dealing directly with customers. Customer care also includes things like hours of detail-oriented work and waiting on hold—monotony that some people embrace and others avoid. Either way, everyone has to accomplish tasks that will support the customer experience in some way.

For every few minutes of solving customers' problems and having them stroke you with gratitude, there is time spent doing the work of putting together orders, pushing them through the system, keying them into computer terminals and waiting for long minutes on the phone.

You can recognize frontline staff with high detail-orientation. They are list makers, and the list guides their day. Their list is prioritized, and they do the hard things first. They feel the happy sensation of closure as they cross a task off their list. They lay awake at night and worry about the things left on their list at the end of their day. They do those things first the next day.

People who aren't detail-oriented genuinely think differently. They can move from day to day without worrying about details, still sleeping well at night. Low detail-oriented people, although they have other strengths, drive high-detail people crazy. Low-detail people tend to think "bigger picture" in terms of people, relationships, team and outcomes. Every organization needs both kinds of people—and both types need to understand what the other brings to the table.

The fact is, every customer-care provider must be prepared to do this kind of detail-oriented work during the majority of his work hours. A job well done, whether it's dealing face-to-face with a customer or a zero-error record for entering data, is to be recognized and rewarded. On any team, you need to have the high-detail people in order to get things accomplished.

Setting standards for achievement in the company should not be based on dealings with customers alone. The more productive you are at the grunt work, the more detail-oriented and error-free, the better the customer experience. It's all part of the great puzzle of how a customer experiences your company. Having a process makes everything easier—easier to stay on track, easier to be thorough, easier to backtrack to discover when things went wrong, easier to follow up and easier to ensure customers are satisfied.

One word of caution about high-detail people. They can create a culture where it is more valued to cross a task off a to-do list than it is to creatively work with customers to solve their problems. There must be a balance between low and high detail. A winning combination when working in customer service is to have a low rules-orientation combined with a high detail-orientation. This leads to an outcome of creatively working with a client, while also making sure all the "t's" are crossed and the "i's" are dotted.

When describing customer service to your frontline staff, make sure they understand that excellence is in this grunt work. Embracing all aspects of the job is part of the delivery of excellence your company expects.

27. HAVE A PROCESS FOR PROBLEM RESOLUTION

Good initiative combined with bad judgment doesn't make for a good customer experience. When a problem needs to be solved but the chosen way to solve it creates more problems, it may be because there is no problem-resolution process in place. Most customer-service providers want to be helpful to their customers but need a proven, repeatable process that will ensure good outcomes on all sides.

Almost every process begins with listening. Without a deep understanding of the problem, we're like a doctor prescribing medicine without a diagnosis. Listening also implies some open, probing questions that give both the customer and the frontline person an opportunity to understand the underlying causes and outcomes of the problem. This allows the customer an opportunity to vent his frustrations. It's important to let him tell his story and not interrupt him unless it's to prompt more information.

Before you can move customers to solvability (a left-brain activity), you need to allow them to get their emotions out (a right-brain activity). If you attempt solvability before they're ready, they will become more emotional and entrenched in anger or frustration.

Next, be sure to reiterate the problem back to them. This is to ensure you heard them correctly, but also to let them know how important it is to you that you heard them and how much you care about what they said. Once you have mutual agreement on the issue, you can move to solving it.

Guilty or innocent, right or wrong, apologize to customers for the inconvenience, frustration and emotional upset. You might be in the right, but your customer is upset and needs to be calmed. Companies are run by people, and it's guaranteed that people will make mistakes. Customers rarely judge service by the mistake. It's the resolution of the mistake that matters to them.

Customer-service providers should try to do as much as possible on their own, but if they do need to bring others in, they should always ask permission of the customer. It engages them and gives them a feeling of control. Keep the customer in the loop every step of the way, and always follow up to ensure the customer is happy and the solution is effective. Follow up is the differentiator that leading companies use to build relationships.

28. HAVE A PROCESS TO WIN BACK GHOSTS

Recently, at lunch with a client in a busy restaurant, I noticed him staring over my shoulder. When questioned, he told me he had just seen a "ghost"—a customer who had been loyal for many years. My client hadn't even realized it, but this customer hadn't placed an order in nearly a year.

"I wonder what happened with him," said my client. "He was a very consistent buyer for so long. Was it something we did? Or worse, something we didn't do?"

"Why don't you ask him?" I said.

With that, he got up from the table and approached his ghost. I didn't see the conversation, but after some time he returned.

"Wow, who knew? He had a pretty bad experience with our service and found a new supplier. We're meeting next week to talk about it."

"Good for you," I replied. "Let's talk about your plan to win him back before that meeting. Don't charge in without a plan of action."

Having a well-thought-out process to win back lost customers yields better results than just trying to sell them something again.

No matter how much you work at winning new business and how you invest in keeping that business, sometimes you will lose some. It may be because of mistakes that have been made, it may be they've been won over by the competition or it may be they just disappear like a ghost in the fog. Whatever the reason, it's crucial that you have a process in place to attempt to win those ghosts back. (That is, if it's the kind of business you want back.) New business is hard fought, and keeping it is a good investment of your time. Having a process in place will give employees a step-by-step way to bring ghosts back into the fold.

Make sure your people understand that when mistakes are made, everything depends on their taking full responsibility. When you have to face a customer and explain a mistake, it is difficult without preparation and a process. For some employees, simply reaching out to a ghost takes courage. Taking responsibility for what has happened takes more courage. A common reason for losing an account is that no one takes ownership of his mistakes. Making excuses is as bad as covering up the problem. Customers rightly believe that if you don't accept responsibility, their problem will likely reoccur.

With responsibility comes the need to learn from your mistakes. Helping ghosts understand the changes you've put in place to avoid future mistakes will help to convince them that the situation won't be repeated in the future. If you want a second chance, they must be assured that they won't experience the problem again. A gentle statement might sound like: "Would you be interested in hearing about the measures we've put in place to avoid future mishaps like this?"

Not every customer will respond positively, and winning customers back may take several tries. Keeping in touch in small ways is important, perhaps even finding opportunities to prove your changes are working. Stop trying and they will forget you. Continue to keep in touch, and you may be rewarded with a second opportunity to serve customers right. It's not the mistakes you make—everyone makes mistakes. It's what you do afterwards that determines your future with a client.

29. HAVE A PROCESS FOR CONTINUOUS IMPROVEMENT

Customer care is a work in progress, and that's a good thing.

You can get a new accounting system and use it for the next five years. You can lease a new office space and expect not to have to paint or upgrade for five years. But with your customer-care system, expect to improve, upgrade, progress, change and innovate on a weekly, if not daily, basis. You are in the process of caring for your customers every minute of every day, and when you're not improving, you can assume the competition is.

When coaching salespeople, company owners and CEOs for forward movement, I often ask them to name the behaviors they had when they first started. What took them to the top originally? Responses often include behaviors like over-the-top service, aggressively prospecting and pure hard work. These behaviors often ebb away in the busyness of workdays.

Lesson learned: The things that took you from zero to 60 can't be left by the roadside. You have to continue to learn, to innovate, to change and to treat each and every one of your customers as if they are the only customer you have and the only person keeping your business's doors open.

Persistence in constant improvement is key. This must include frontline employees' knowledge and implementation of best practices and service standards. It also includes monitoring for consistency. Improvement is a belief system that begins at the top of an organization and permeates the company through its constant presence. Bad habits lurk around every corner and can quickly take hold.

Success doesn't happen overnight. It is a constant journey through failure, mistakes, criticism, time and struggle to get it right and keep it right. A willingness to continue to focus on customer service once you reach success is what differentiates the average companies from the industry leaders.

Fostering company passion for customer care is not a onetime endeavor, but an ongoing, institutionalized focus that must be part of the yearly execution of your goals and plan. You are never "there."

Steal from the Best

So many of the best practices in customer service are learned from observing others who do it well. Sometimes, too, it's a lesson learned on what not to do from those who do it badly. Either way, it's valuable information and fodder for developing best practices for your organization. Here is a checklist of behaviors that you might keep in mind when choosing with whom you will do business:

- Were they welcoming to you, not just with rote words, but with natural body language and genuine tonality?
- Did they quickly personalize the engagement by learning and using your name?

- Did they ask compelling questions to uncover what you needed, particularly why and when you needed it?
- Were they helpful in providing or putting you in touch with information that you needed?
- Were you completely comfortable sharing information with them that would help them to help you?
- Did they leave you with definite next steps, timelines, expectations and outcomes?
- Did the overall experience make you feel like it was a place you would like to do business?
- Was every interaction with the company consistently high in quality?

If you can answer "yes" to these questions, observe and pay very close attention to each interaction you have with that company. You can learn from them. You will need to lay down a strategy to close the gap between where you are now and where you need to take your people and your company.

Avoid the "Flavor of the Month"

My friend Jill has five young children—all girls. She attends parenting classes sometimes, but each time she does she arrives home with a whole new strategy to get her children and her household in line. Her strategy is backfiring lately because each new idea is met with a roll of her daughters' eyes and a "what's the flavor of the month now?" attitude. Her effectiveness is diminished by bouncing around from the newest/latest idea to the next newest/latest. Choose a system and stick with it; practice and improve on it, but don't throw it over for the next "shiny object" that comes along.

CHAPTER 8

Sandler Rules for Finding Sales Opportunities

Customer care often means connecting customers with new products and services. Having an approach and process will differentiate you from your competition. Here are some rules:

30. Expect resistance and meet it with an attitude shift.
31. Use the helping approach to growing business.
32. Selling is something you do with a customer, not to a customer.
33. Understand the value of one customer.
34. Teach an outbound calling process, not a script.
35. Become an opportunity finder.

36. Make time for business development.
37. Sell value, not price.
38. Check for icebergs.
39. Stop up-selling; instead, extreme up-serve.

Most owners will tell you that it's everybody's job in the company to sell. That's true for all frontline service providers—if not to sell, at the very least, to recognize opportunities and alert the sales department.

Anyone who touches the customer in any way is in a position to recognize selling opportunities. "It's not my job" just doesn't fly anymore. Everyone's job security depends upon taking advantage of every sales opportunity. Having "sales antennae" and recognizing buying signals is something that can be trained.

The problem is, the many tech specialists would probably think: "Sales—that's not my job." They're right of course, but their job is to help the customer. Part of helping is connecting customers to the people who can deliver what they need to solve their problem. If you are not a salesperson, you are a connector to the salesperson. It is your job to put the client in touch with the sales representative.

Training frontline people in sales is not to make them into prospecting salespeople. But they should be able to question for need, understand value, recognize and find opportunities, ask compelling questions and recognize buying signals. They should not be afraid of selling or have a negative mindset around sales. Training must be tailored to suit their jobs, but helping them outside their comfort zone is a good way to build confidence and growth in your frontline employees.

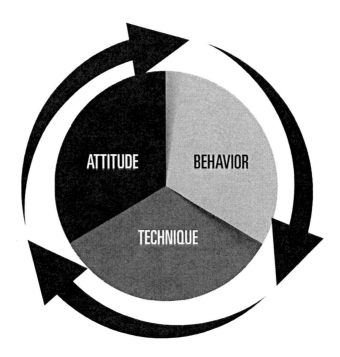

There are three components that must be assembled to ensure customer-care providers can and will sell. Their attitude has to be right—they must understand that they are not nagging, cajoling, pleading or bullying customers into buying. They are helping them to make good buying decisions. Next, customer-care providers need a set of behaviors that reflects a helping attitude—questioning techniques, qualifying criteria and a way of building commitment with the customers. Finally, they need a schedule of behaviors to ensure consistent use of those winning techniques that will result in sales.

30. EXPECT RESISTANCE AND MEET IT WITH AN ATTITUDE SHIFT

David Sandler was a student of human nature, particularly when it came to sales. He understood that there were parts of sales that many saw as intrusive, manipulative or aggressive. He created his selling system to be a complete disclosure—an open, honest and thorough process of discovery to ensure that neither seller nor buyer felt pushed or manipulated. Thousands have benefited from his step-by-step process of helping customers get exactly what they need.

Like most people, customer-care providers often have a preconceived notion of what sales is all about that flies in the face of helping customers. They believe the definition of selling is getting prospects to buy something they don't need or want. Like the line from the movie *Tommy Boy*, "He could sell a ketchup Popsicle to a woman in white gloves." This attitude puts sales outside the zone of commitment to helping customers get what they want.

The resistance you feel when you ask a customer-care person to sell is rooted in his belief system, and no amount of coaxing will change that. Wouldn't it be better to help customer-care providers step outside their comfort zone by providing a set of behaviors (i.e., a selling system) that is the antithesis of their belief system about salespeople?

Personal growth happens when you step outside your comfort zone and do something you're afraid of doing. Many years ago, I set a goal of running the annual 10k in my hometown. I am in no way naturally athletic, not built for speed and, embarrassingly, the slowest runner ever. However, I trained and showed up on May 1.

The first year, a man on crutches with one leg beat me. The next, the police were picking up the pylons as I jogged by. Each year I have finished in the bottom ten percent, but each year I beat my previous year's finishing time and became more and more comfortable with changing what I saw as a "failure" to a new attitude. I accomplished my goal, I continue to grow healthier and I beat the 300,000 people who stayed in bed that morning. Victory!

Stepping outside one's comfort zones into a sales role is daunting and fearful. But given goals, support, training and a process, it can be fulfilling—and even fun. Your people will increase their self-esteem if given an opportunity to grow their skills in the area of sales. Accomplishment of a difficult goal can make you overcome fears and build both confidence and competence. If your customer-care providers have been comfortable for too long, it makes it harder and harder to break out of the prison that is their comfort zone.

Don't Take It Personally

One of the key areas of discomfort for customer-care providers is repeated criticism, negativity and blame. They seldom realize this is not aimed at them personally but at their company or their role. Customers will often try to make it personal ("You don't seem to know what you're doing!"), but this is a tactic they use to get either movement on a problem or concessions.

Whatever the reason, frontline people who don't learn the difference between their self-identity and their role will find their self-esteem dip every time they experience a confrontational customer. Burnout is a possibility if they do not understand that they can't take it personally.

Build Self-Esteem

Develop your people by giving them new challenges and goals to meet in the area of sales. Ensure that you also give them the tools and encouragement it takes to push past self-doubt and reach their goals.

31. USE THE HELPING APPROACH TO GROWING BUSINESS

The great advantage customer-service providers have in the business development area is that they are there to help. Customers see them as helpful, and often what they need help with is making good buying decisions. Buyers often hold a negative or at least skeptical view of salespeople—"They're just trying to sell me something." This is not the same with customer-care providers, particularly when there is a long-term relationship that has been helpful many times in the past.

Truthfully, customer-care providers can provide help to their customers by selling them products and services that improve their life, make their jobs easier, save them money or make them more productive. But part of the problem is between the customer-service providers' ears—they don't believe they're salespeople.

Customer-service providers must realize how helpful introducing products and services can be. Naturally, if a buyer doesn't need the product or service, don't sell it to him. But you can only uncover a need by asking the right questions.

Often buyers don't know what they want or need. For example, an insurance agent recently discovered that a farmer's barn was only insured for the original value. A barn built 40 years ago has a replacement value of many times the original cost. The farmer was unaware of this until the competitive agent brought it to his attention; he realized he might be put out of business if he had to borrow the cost to replace that barn fully. The value brought to the farmer was more than a new policy. It was an agent who cared and looked to his client's best interests. Was he trying to sell something? Or was he trying to help? The answer is, "Yes."

Fear, Uncertainty and Doubt

FUD, or "fear, uncertainty and doubt" (the original computer term), was used to describe the subconscious anxiety causing users to choose safety over change. When asked to sell, some customer-care providers are plunged into that same cycle of fear, uncertainty and doubt. They display their discomfort with either excuses ("I'm too busy with incoming or present customers") or avoidance ("I'll do it tomorrow") behavior. Give customer-care providers the right attitude, tools, process and behavior guide, and they will replace that fear, uncertainty and doubt, leading to better outcomes, confidence and self-esteem.

People Buy in Spite of the Hard Sell, Not Because of It

Joe Junior was the son of the owner of the furniture store in our local mall. Joe started working there right out of high school and gradually worked his way up to selling on the floor. One day as I browsed through the store looking for a specific item, I saw Joe making a bee-line toward me. He asked me how I was today and what I needed. He smothered me for the next few minutes with information on specials, products and next-day delivery. Joe was too full of information, too anxious to please, too smothering for me. He quite literally drove me out of the store in his desperation to make a sale.

As I fled, I glanced over at Joe Senior. The smile on his face said, "That's my boy. Sell everyone who comes in the store!" Unfortunately for Joe Junior, he had taken all his cues on how to sell and serve customers from someone who was stuck in the 1960s. He had no idea that, rather than smother me, a few well-placed questions would have pulled me in rather than push me away. If he'd asked me a question and waited for the answer, I might have explained why I was there and he might have been able to help me. But he was too busy telling me every feature and benefit of the store and products. It was all about him—giving me the hard sell.

Whether you are making calls to introduce a new product, calling in to check on inventory levels or refreshing relationships that have drifted away, bringing products and services to the buyer's attention is an important part of business for both you and the buyer. This is part of a buyer's decision-making process. You can be a part of that process by establishing your credibility through thoughtful questions and helping him make a good buying decision.

32. SELLING IS SOMETHING YOU DO WITH A CUSTOMER, NOT TO A CUSTOMER

Carol was brand new to sales, but her supervisor had seen a drive and determination in her that no one else in the service department seemed to have. He gave her an opportunity to develop new business with some of the company's present customers. Daily she brought her persuasive skills to bear on her prospects, explaining in detail why they should buy her software bundle over the competition. But for all the effort she was putting in, she was disappointed in the results. They weren't getting better; in fact they were getting worse each day.

One weekend while visiting her family ranch, she watched as her father put a herd of thoroughbred horses into a pasture.

Rather than put a rope around each one's neck and pull it toward the gate, he gently put his hand on the rump of the lead horse. The horse effortlessly moved forward toward the new pasture. The other horses followed, unafraid.

She asked him, "What would he have done if you'd pulled him in, Dad?"

"You know the answer to that, Carol. He would have dug his heels in and not budged an inch. I'm strong, but not that strong."

"Thanks, Dad, I think I know what I've been doing wrong in sales!"

The next week, Carol changed her phone tactics. She gently got behind her prospects the way her father had gotten behind the horse. Instead of pulling them toward a sale with features and benefits, making them nervous and distrustful, she gently asked questions about what they had, what they needed and what they didn't need, never mentioning a feature or benefit. She could feel the trust building with her prospects. More importantly, she began to have better outcomes—for herself, her company and her prospects.

Pulling a prospect toward *yes* creates the same reaction as it does in high-performance thoroughbreds. It creates resistance. Customers can't be pulled toward a sale without creating resistance. Customer-service providers recognize that resistance instantly. They take it as a *no* when really it is the result of their approach. Like the rancher, too often they get between the customer and the sale!

Customer-care providers often have a skewed view of what selling is about and worry that they must be aggressive and pushy to browbeat customers into buying. Nothing is further from the truth. In fact, frontline employees probably sell more by simply helping their customers. Helping implies that you are making suggestions to make customers' work easier, increase their sales or make their businesses run better.

In customer care, the secret is not to repeat a list of everything that the company sells. It's to ask questions that uncover the needs customers may have and then make the connection between how you can help with those uncovered needs. When a customer discovers his own needs, it is much more powerful than you telling him, "You're going to love this. You should have one of these." No one likes having things told to him. When you tell, you set barriers. When frontline staff members understand they don't have to be pushy, overbearing or aggressive, they are much more likely to perform the behaviors that will help their customers discover their needs.

Here are sample questions: "Do you often have to shut down your production line because of paper jams?" "Are long back-order waits causing problems for your customers?" "Are you concerned about meeting the new federal regulations for safety on time?"

A true professional helps buyers sort through their alternatives and finds the best fit for their needs and their budget. Good salespeople become a resource for matching a buyer's problem with a great solution. They help their customers improve their business and processes, and they make their lives easier.

Customer-service providers are hired to help customers get what they need. When what the customer needs is not immediately apparent, the process by which the customer-service providers render that help is called sales. Selling is the process by which the seller helps the buyer make great buying decisions. Sales is something you do with a customer, not to a customer.

Learn to ask questions about customers' needs and wants, rather than smothering them with the features and benefits of your products and services. The old approach of, "What can I convince you to buy from me?" has been replaced with a customer-focused, "Tell me about your needs today."

You can't sell anybody anything. But you can help your customers make good buying decisions.

33. UNDERSTAND THE VALUE OF ONE CUSTOMER

David sat grimacing in the customer-care meeting Monday morning. "I don't see why we have to deal with Frank Smith at ABC. That account takes as much time as two other accounts. And Frank is so picky; he criticizes everything we do. Do we really need accounts like that?"

David's supervisor Eric thought for a moment, and then they had this conversation:

Eric: Well, let's see what that account is worth, Dave. What is his average sale?

David: I guess around $250.

Eric: I see, and how many times a month does he buy?

David: Three, maybe four times.

Eric: OK, let's say three times, that's $750 per month, right? Does he do that every month?

David: Yes.

Eric: OK, then that's $9,000 per year. How many years has he been dealing with us?

David: A long time, maybe 20 years.

Eric: So $9,000 times 20 would make it about $180,000. Do you think he'll continue to buy for another ten years if we treat him right?

David: Sure.

Eric: Well, that's another $90,000. Add that to the last 20 years, and we're up to $270,000. Has Frank ever given us referrals?

David: Actually, he gave me one only the other day. He's pretty good like that. I can think of many customers who came to us through Frank.

Eric: So, let's say Frank gives us one referral per year, who buys the same $250 as regularly as he buys. Over the same period of 30 years, that would give additional revenue of about $8,000,000.

David: What? I guess we should keep Frank around then!

Eric: Yes, I think we'll keep Frank around. Matter of fact, let's send him a little something. I know he plays golf. Shall we send him a couple of golf games on us?

David: I'm on it!

Every customer is important. To understand each customer's value, use the same formula that Eric used.

Frontline service providers need to understand the value of one customer. It's a simple mathematical formula, but the lesson it brings home to employees is invaluable.

Start with your average sale and multiply that by the number of purchases per year the average customer will make. Multiply that total by the average number of years you keep a customer.

Next, calculate the number of referrals you may get from that customer in a year and add those to the total of that one customer. What follows here is the calculation. Use it to figure out what the average lifetime value of one customer is in your world. This number never fails to astound frontline service providers. They come to see that every single customer is critical to the company and is more than the one call they didn't return or the one email they left unanswered.

Every customer is critical to the success of the company. Fill in the blanks to this formula to discover what each customer means financially to your company.

Average sale	(A)	_____
Number of sales per month per customer	(B)	_____
Monthly income from one customer (A×B)	(C)	_____
Yearly income from one customer (C×12)	(D)	_____
Number of years of loyalty from customer	(E)	_____
Value over those years (E×D)	(F)	_____
Number of referrals from one customer/year	(G)	_____
Value of those referrals (G×F)	(K)	_____
Total value of one customer (K+F)	(Total)	_____

This number brings home both the value of customer loyalty and the additional numbers that good service can provide through referrals. These can be directly attributed to the customer-service provider's behaviors and attitudes and become a motivator.

34. TEACH AN OUTBOUND CALLING PROCESS, NOT A SCRIPT

The problem with most over-the-phone salespeople is that they do what comes naturally instead of what works. They sound like a traditional salesperson just trying to sell something, and this brings out resistance in clients or prospects. This resistance or defensiveness is a natural protective reaction, but it creates a wall that many customer-care providers can't penetrate.

Where does this defensiveness originate? It comes from their experience with outbound callers who:

- Don't explain the purpose of the call.
- Take up too much of their valuable time.
- Feel trapped into saying "yes," when they want to say "no."
- Believe that salespeople have their own agenda and don't care about the clients.
- Are not kept informed about the outcomes of the conversation.

The way around this defensiveness is as simple as Sandler's Up-Front Contract. This technique can take only seconds but establishes a comfort level for the client, control for the customer-service provider and better outcomes for both.

Here's an example of a pared down up-front contract:

"John, do you mind if I take 20 seconds to tell you why I called? If you're interested, we can have a conversation. If you're not, you can tell me and we'll end the call right there."

You've covered several concerns here. The customer understands how long you will take. He doesn't feel trapped into saying "yes" because you've given him permission to say "no." You've provided an escape hatch for him. The pressure is off, and he's more likely to say, "Yes, go ahead."

Let's look at a longer version of an up-front contract.

Time and Purpose

"Hi, John, thanks for taking my call. When we spoke on Friday you asked me to call you back this morning at 10:00. Do you have about 15 minutes to exchange information to see if this new product is a fit or not?"

Customer's Agenda and Your Agenda

"I assume you'll want to know what most people ask me: Is there any retrofitting required, what's the investment and how long does it take to install? Anything else we should cover? I'll need to gather some information on what you're using now to make sure it is applicable."

Outcomes and Mutual Agreement

"By the end of our 15 minutes, will you be comfortable saying, 'No, thanks,' or 'Let's go ahead'? Great."

This version covers all the concerns clients often have when taking a sales call. Like any contract, the mutual agreement seals the deal. If they don't agree to the process, it's best to find out beforehand why.

35. BECOME AN OPPORTUNITY FINDER

Part of the attitude shift to developing new business with a customer is understanding that the job is not to sell somebody something. It is to gather the information that will tell you if the customer needs what you have, and if so, to determine how important it is to him. This is a skill that combines the art of preparing compelling questions that dig into his challenges and roadblocks with that of questioning so that he self-discovers that he needs what you have to offer. When a customer-care person tries to "sell" a customer on a great product or service, he sounds self-serving and suspect. But when a customer presents a problem he knows needs to be fixed, you are simply helping him move his business forward.

You've probably heard the term "recognizing an opportunity when you see one." It is a passive term referring to an ability to recognize the buying signals of a customer. But it is passive. Customer-care providers who can ask the questions that uncover an opportunity deliver benefits to both the customer and your company. Here's an example:

> "Mr. Jones, I see that last year you nearly doubled your widget order in the month of January, and most of those were 'rush' orders. Can I ask you what happened there? Might that be the case again this month? Would it make sense to stock more in December this year so you wouldn't have to pay the overnight shipping fees?"

Sometimes it may pay off, sometimes not, but either way, the customer understands that you are more than an order-taker. You have his best interests at heart, and you are looking at his long-term benefits.

Asking good questions in the right way is the key to finding opportunities. For example: "I don't suppose you'll need a case to protect that from the rain, will you?" "You've had us fix this twice in the last month. Might it be time to replace it?" "Is it awkward to pick this up every week? Would you like to hear about our automatic delivery system?"

If the question is of interest to the customer or he sees the benefits, he will let you know. On the other hand, if he sees an agenda for your benefit, he will shy away. Becoming an opportunity finder brings value to customers and the company.

36. MAKE TIME FOR BUSINESS DEVELOPMENT

John was quietly worrying at his desk. He was the top customer-care provider in his company for the last seven years running. He knew hundreds of customers by name and most asked for him when they called. But his boss had come to him that week and asked him to make 200 outgoing calls to new prospects about a new product introduction. This wasn't what John signed up for—he was never told he would have to make outbound calls, much less sell! He was so busy with his inbound customers he couldn't possibly make that many calls anyway. It didn't make sense to him to ignore present customers just to make calls to prospects who probably wouldn't buy from him anyway. John felt stuck. If he refused to do the calls, it would look bad. If he took time away from his customers, he would feel bad. John decided to put off the calls as long as possible. His boss would see things his way. John was surprised when that wasn't the case.

Resistance to sales responsibilities often means procrastination. Customer-care providers need to make the time to sell each day. In other words, they need to schedule it into their workday just like they would an important meeting, a doctor's appointment or a day off. The nature of the job for frontline people requires them to be immediately responsive to customers. It's difficult to set time aside for outbound calls, but if it is truly a priority it can be done.

"I was so busy, I didn't get time to do my calls today," is a familiar cry. If those calls are scheduled from 9:00 A.M. to 9:45 A.M. and the frontline workers have someone to cover their desk or phones, it will be accomplished. Having a block of time dedicated to the task ensures that they won't be pulled away mid-task and not get back to it. The block removes many excuses. Naturally there are sometimes emergencies that do pull employees away. But a regularly scheduled time to form a habit and sales muscles can be developed and is the most productive format.

Structured time takes the decision making out of prospecting. If something is scheduled for 9:00, then at 9:00 you start. It's not a question of, "Do I feel like doing it?" or "Is this the best time to do it?" or "Is there something more important I can do?" It's scheduled, so it's time to do it—now. Customer-care and inside salespeople can think of it as a time to reach out to either new prospects or present customers to see what help they may need. The rewards of helping customers make the time investment well worth their while.

Structuring the time is the first step. Customer-care providers also need to know what to say to prospects. This may or may not mean a script. They may be comfortable with a script, but a script can never provide an answer to every question or every reply from a customer. It's better to prepare them with an outline and a conceptual approach. At Sandler, it's a skeleton format and a questioning line that we call qualifying.

Many customer-care providers have sales responsibilities, targets and metrics. Traditionally there is a dollar-sign goal at the end of each day, week, month or quarter, as the success and future of any enterprise depends on revenue and a balance sheet. The problem is that many companies work on the wrong end of the problem—the outcomes—rather than the behaviors that achieve those outcomes.

The problem with tracking only the money is that it's difficult to pinpoint where sales get off track when you only see the outcomes. It can also create undue pressure on frontline staff and customers. For example, as the end of the week approaches and inside people have not yet hit their numbers, the phone calls tend to sound more desperate and more self-centered.

You must first discover if there is a training or a coaching issue. Do your frontline people have a proven, repeatable process to contact and sell their customers? Can they become comfortable and successful with this process? If not, training is a starting place.

Next, are there clearly defined metrics and expectations set up with your frontline people? Do they understand how many calls need to be made to reach their goals? Do they understand the purpose of the calls? Can they identify what constitutes a successful outcome? Do they have a form of accountability so they don't procrastinate or fall hopelessly behind? Are you checking in with them consistently to ensure they get support, constantly improve and make the adjustments they may need to be successful? If they know what to do but for some reason aren't executing it, that's a coaching situation.

When you identify the goals and understand the behaviors required to reach and quantify those goals, it creates internal motivation to satisfy those goals. Set the bar too high, however, and it becomes a de-motivator. Set goals just above expectations and employees will strive to meet or even exceed them.

Here's an example of a tracking process:

BEHAVIOR	M	T	W	T	F	TOTAL
New Dials	10	10	10	10	10	50
Talks	6	6	6	6	6	30
Demos	2	2	2	2	2	10
Follow Ups	2	1	2	1	2	8
Inbound Calls	10	10	8	8	8	44
Sales	2	1	2	2	2	9

If money is not a natural outcome of tracked behaviors, then there's an issue with the behavior. It may be time to rethink how you're behaving for more productive results.

If the process is good, perhaps the numbers are just too low (which would require more new dials per day). If customer-service providers are telling you they spend too much time on inbound calls to be able to perform outbound calls, it may be a time-management issue or perhaps the system is too arduous to complete the sale in a timely manner and you need to rethink the process.

For customer-service providers, developing new business may not be what they expected as part of their job when they were hired. You can't simply tack it on to their responsibilities and expect that it will be done correctly. It needs to be a defined process that you can track, adjust and grow. Otherwise, you have busy but not productive employees.

Being held accountable for daily behaviors is something that often meets resistance. But most customer-care providers will be happy to have a defined process and clear expectations. Accountability is effective if it is used as a learning process, not a stick to punish employees.

37. SELL VALUE, NOT PRICE

Customer-care providers typically know the price of everything in the company. What they don't always grasp is the value that the products, the services and they themselves bring to customers. They believe that the lowest price always gets the sale, and they feel pressure from customers to deliver on that lowest price. In fact, they will pressure management or use price as an excuse for why customers leave. The truth is that customers seldom leave over price. More often they leave because they feel taken for granted or neglected. The service they receive has value to customers, and they understand there is a price tag attached to that.

"You know what the Internet store is selling this for right now?" John said to explain to his boss why his clients weren't interested in the company's new widgets. "No one will pay our price once they see the Internet store's price! There's no point in making those calls. Once they see that price, they'll think we're gouging them; they'll think we're just greedy! Now, if I could price match, they might be interested."

"John, you know what makes our widget different from the Internet store's widget?"

"Sure," said John. "It lasts 50 percent longer."

"Do you know what that means for our customers?"

"I guess it means there would be fewer work stoppages to fix broken widgets."

"What do you think that would save our customers in lost time, loss of productivity and slower customer service?"

"I don't know, probably thousands of dollars."

"Do you still think the competition's price is the best one?"

"But customers don't understand that difference. All they're interested in is the price!"

"Whose job is it to focus our customers on the value, not the price?"

"Mine?"

"You've got it! We've got the best product and the best service. We have to help our customers recognize that. Let's figure out an approach on the phone that will help us do just that."

Customers have trained companies to constantly be the "low price leader" by constantly playing them off their competition and using veiled threats and bullying tactics to lower prices. But customers also understand that better value (longer lasting, higher quality, better performance, better after-sale service) has a price tag, and they are often willing to pay that price. It is your job to help them self-discover the value of your products and services. They only use price to compare you to your competition if they don't understand the return on investment that buying your products and services will give them.

Customer-service providers who understand the value of the goods and services they sell and what they themselves bring to the customer will not be afraid of the prospect who says, "I can get it for $5 less across the street." They'll have the confidence and training to ask questions to uncover the $100 return they'll get if they invest that extra $5.

38. CHECK FOR ICEBERGS

Icebergs are reputed to have ten percent of their mass visible above the water line, with the other 90 percent of their bulk below, hidden from view. Customers are often the same—only ten percent of their needs are apparent, even to them. Although they may hold back information, often they haven't thought the entire issue through logically and analytically and don't know the extent of their needs.

In order to address the customer's real needs, you have to reveal the unseen part of the iceberg for him. Looking beyond his immediate need to the reason behind it is up-serving at its best.

Physicist Albert Einstein once said: "I am neither especially clever nor especially gifted. I am only very, very curious." It's a great gift to be able to explore and understand the 90 percent of the iceberg unseen by others' eyes. Digging deeper into customer issues is the greatest differentiator you can have. Your competition is satisfied with the first explanation the customer gives and immediately jumps to satisfying the presented issue. But customers don't always understand the source of the problem. You may be trying to fix the wrong issue. The problem the customer brings you is never the real problem. There's almost always something deeper at the source that is causing the symptoms they present.

A customer arrives to buy a bag of widgets. He says he needs them right away. You can sell him the bag of widgets, or you can have this conversation with him:

You: That's a lot of widgets. Do you mind if I ask you a question? Why so many at once?

Customer: They get sheared off on the production line. We have to stop a couple times a day to replace them to keep the line going.

You: Whoa—how long does that take you?

Customer: About 30 minutes each time.

You: I don't suppose that's affecting productivity?

Customer: That's why I'm here buying all these widgets!

You: You know, about 80 percent of the time shearing is caused by a misaligned line that shears pins off. Would you be interested in seeing a fix for that misalignment?

Customer: Probably costs an arm and a leg and takes two weeks to fix, doesn't it?

You: Not at all. But how much time and expense are you investing now with no permanent solution?

Customer: Let me have a look. I do need to get this fixed.

Is this selling? Yes. Is this up-serving? Yes. Any time you can make your customers' jobs easier, saving them time or money, you can be assured you are selling/helping. Is every interaction with a customer a potential up-sell? Maybe not, but there's only one way to be sure what is and what isn't, and that's to assume everything is an iceberg and to ask the right questions.

Curiosity leads to underlying causes, ideas, better solutions and success. Sometimes you succumb to your own *head trash* (faulty belief systems) about how many questions you can ask a customer before annoying him. Don't allow a fear of intrusiveness or time limitations stop you from getting to a customer's real problems. Customers don't mind being asked questions; in fact, they appreciate it, as it helps them crystallize their thinking and understand their own needs.

39. STOP UP-SELLING; INSTEAD, EXTREME UP-SERVE

If you are doing a good job matching customers' needs to your products or services, there is really no need to up-sell or cross-sell. Doing a good job means that you have asked all the questions about what they want, why they want it, how they will be using it, why they want that particular one, what they've heard about it, what their budget is, how they'll make a decision to buy, etc. When you thoroughly understand their needs and have asked all your questions, you should be able to offer a solution that exactly fits their needs. This will fit all the pieces of the puzzle together to ensure they're happy.

The problem with adding on more expense after selling the main item is that you run the risk of taking the customer out of his comfort zone financially or having him feel pushed into something he didn't need or want.

Buyers are more sophisticated than ever. They recognize and feel the pressure from the obvious signs of up-selling and cross-selling. They often see this not as an attempt to help them get the most use from their product or services, but as an attempt to squeeze additional dollars out of them for the seller's profit.

This is not to say they shouldn't have all the pieces of the puzzle that will help them enjoy the most usage from their new product or services. However, those pieces should be sold to them as part of the discovery process of how they'll use it, not as add-ons to the original price.

Find out what the customers need and sell them that. Don't catch their interest with a lower price point, and then try to persuade them they want a higher-priced item. You will come across as unethical and self-interested. Open and honest communication is a differentiator in today's marketplace and is appreciated by most discerning buyers.

Forget the up-sell. Extreme up-serve instead.

CHAPTER 9

Sandler Rules for Up-Serving

There are service levels that establish your position in the market, customer loyalty and word-of-mouth sales growth. The basic level that most companies comply with includes getting customer invoices out on time, having satisfactory delivery times and doing well enough to stay in business. Next, there are "industry standards," which deliver more personalized service, friendly smiling faces on the service desk and knowledgeable service providers. But there is a level beyond that which sets some companies apart from the crowd. Up-serving companies believe that nothing is more important than serving and satisfying their customers.

Companies like L.L. Bean, Starbucks, Samsung, Lowe's, Marks and Spencer and Enterprise Rent-A-Car have been up-serving for years, and it has propelled them into first-in-class positions. This status reflects quality, helpfulness, how they handle problems, how well staff is trained and whether or not customers are treated as valued guests.

40. Make customer service job number one.
41. Sweat the small stuff.
42. Encourage ownership.
43. To keep your customers, treat them like you don't have them yet.
44. Do more than you're paid for.
45. Fix problems before they happen.
46. Allow customers to ring the bell.
47. Keep in touch to keep relationships.
48. Engage customers on an emotional level.

40. MAKE CUSTOMER SERVICE JOB NUMBER ONE

Every company is in business for one reason: to deliver a product or service to a customer in exchange for compensation. However, many company leaders fail to communicate the priority of customer care to frontline staff. Internal processes, billing problems and warehouse and shipping issues all must be seen within the context of how they affect customer relationships.

John was in early on Monday to restock the store shelves. He started at 4:00 A.M. in order to be ready for the 9:00 A.M. door opening, but this day he couldn't get to every department. By the time the doors were open, stock was piled in the back room and some shelves were barely half full. Worse, customers were continually stopping him and asking questions. If this continued, he'd have to punch in overtime just to catch up.

He ducked out of the aisle when he saw another customer headed his way. John suddenly realized the absurdity of avoiding customers and, embarrassed, realized that customers were the reason he had a job. He set aside his goal of getting out on time that day and helped customers locate what they needed. Restocking could wait.

Connecting a customer to the right product and services is key. For companies, the payoff is loyalty, customer engagement, sales results, growth potential and top-line outcomes. Ralph Waldo Emerson wrote, "It is one of the beautiful compensations of this life that no man can sincerely try to help another without helping himself." That's just another way of saying that you reap what you sow. Applying Emerson to customer service, what you invest in a customer in time and nurturing, you get back in sales and loyalty.

This is a statement of position. It speaks to how customers are prioritized and the business model chosen. You will fulfill all the needs you have if you ensure your customers' needs are met. It's a natural outcome. Make the customers' problems your problems. When you solve their problems or meet their needs in some way, you create a partnership. Partnerships give a sense of belonging.

The customer becomes a part of something that is helpful and meaningful to him. People have a need to belong.

Start and continue to make customers' satisfaction the one key success goal and indicator. Begin to build your people, your systems and your company around that single clarified statement. You'll reach your goals.

As companies grow, they try to scale their personal touch with customers. Often rules are established instead of culture. On the front lines, following the rules is alienating, whereas being part of, and believing in, a customer-focused culture is empowering—and rewarding!

You cannot write a policy manual that covers every situation a frontline employee will face. In fact, you can't even definitely say what excellent customer service is! But by clearly communicating that customers are job number one and that excellent service is recognized and rewarded, even without a rulebook employees will know what to do. Training, modeling and inspiring by management's example, reinforcement and reward will keep customer-focus fresh in everyone's mind constantly.

Try challenging your frontline staff to find five ways to exceed customer expectations—three individually and two as an organization. To ensure this is not just an exercise, set up a rewards or recognition system for implementation.

Up-serving means there is nothing more important in your company than serving and satisfying your customer.

41. SWEAT THE SMALL STUFF

Like actors on the stage, every role is critical, no matter how many lines you have. Everything you do in the service of your customers is important. Every role makes up part of their entire experience with your company. Every detail is important. In fact, it's the small details that can make or break customer service.

A burned-out light or a stain on the carpet may seem trivial to you, or you may be so used to them that you no longer notice they're there. But by not addressing these things, you are effectively telling customers that their opinions don't matter to you. There is a real psychological impact to dirty windows, broken signage and stained furniture. You can't convince customers (and staff) that you value them if you aren't making their surroundings comfortable and pleasing.

In customer service, small things matter. Small things, like getting a real person on the phone instead of a voicemail maze or being greeted by a well-trained employee, send the message that you respect and care about your employees and customers.

Delayed billing might seem like a little thing to you, but if your customer's accountant is delaying his year-end because of it, it has a huge impact. It's your attentiveness to these little things that says to your customers: "Your problems are our problems, and we want to make your life easier, not harder. How can we help?"

A great example of a company that "sweats the small stuff" is Starbucks. When they take your order, they ask your name and write it on your cup. It's a small thing that accomplishes two goals. First, it ensures you get your exact order; second, they establish a personal connection when you order ("Thanks, Mary, it will be ready at the next counter in two minutes.") and when the order is ready (they'll call "Mary!"). The name is uttered twice and is music to the customer's ears.

A small detail with a big impact.

What are the little things in your organization that need to be fixed to prove you care? Challenge your frontline staff to come up with a Top 10 Priority List and begin the process of constant improvement with the small stuff.

42. ENCOURAGE OWNERSHIP

I know the sign over my workplace door says "Sandler Training," but when I'm working with a customer, it's "MacKeigan Training." I own the relationship, the products or service, the customer experience and the future of that relationship. While I'm working, it's my company. It's my name and reputation on the line. I am a trainer, but I'm in the business of serving customers. My success is completely dependent on their success.

Ownership is a form of taking personal responsibility for any transactions that may cross your path each day. The most important relationship you have is not with your boss or with the accounting department; it's with the purchaser of your products and services. Customers go by different names and different roles. They may have a title like "buyer," or they may be the head of human resources or the custodian mopping the floor, but they all make decisions on what to buy and where to buy it. The decision path may involve more than one person but, whoever they are, you are serving them.

It is never anybody else's fault; it's never the driver's fault or someone in the warehouse—it's me. I'm the one who owns the contract with the customer who calls in, emails, visits our website or walks through the door. If the customer speaks to me first, I am responsible for seeing him through to satisfaction.

When you pass a difficult customer off to another, you abdicate your responsibility and your opportunity. Every customer gives you an opportunity to build the relationship, practice your skills and grow your business. You must own their dissatisfaction, their frustrations and their solutions.

If serving others is seen as beneath you, an interruption in your day or a bother, you are in the wrong business. If you are on the front lines of any organization, you are there to serve the customer and ensure his satisfaction and, hopefully, his delight. You're there to make his day better, his job easier and his load lighter. Owning his issues will lighten that load immediately. Solving them will make the load disappear, with loyalty and delight taking its place.

Up-serving differentiates you by never using blame, never shifting responsibility, never having an excuse. The only words a customer wants to hear are: "I should have checked," and "How can I make this right?"

43. TO KEEP YOUR CUSTOMERS, TREAT THEM LIKE YOU DON'T HAVE THEM YET

No one likes to be taken for granted, particularly loyal customers. Often companies try to entice new customers with offers that aren't available to present customers. This sends a message about who is important and who is not. A general rule of thumb says that 80 percent of your business comes from 20 percent of your customers. The rest of your customers may have the potential to grow into high-value customers. Don't you value and need all customers to be successful?

Hold regular events like "Customer Appreciation Days" or send a handwritten thank-you note after any order. At the very least, a regular phone call of appreciation (not weekly, but every couple of months at least) will maintain the strong connection. Be sure to ask them if there's anything you could be doing differently to better serve them. This is not a sales call, so don't ask them to buy more. It's a relationship call that sends the message, "We're glad you chose us."

"Marion, do you realize you have someone waiting on hold?" asked Tom.

"Oh, that's Dave. I don't think he'll mind waiting."

Tom was shocked. Dave was one of their most loyal

customers and had been for years. Tom picked up the extension and apologized for keeping Dave waiting and asked how he could help. He quickly placed Dave's order and added, "Shipping will be free on this one, Dave. We really appreciate your patience and your order, and I apologize again for keeping you waiting."

Tom realized that they spent too little time keeping the customers they have, and he had put too much emphasis on new customer acquisition with his customer-service group. Losing a loyal customer like Dave through neglect might have been a costly mistake.

If you take your present customers for granted, they will feel it and act accordingly.

Bend over backwards to help the people you serve. This begins with your attitude. Do you care about the quality of the job you do each day, the products you put out into the marketplace, the service you supply, the relationships you build and the image you have in your marketplace? Attitude starts at your belief system. It helps if your belief system starts with the fact that your customers are the reason—the only reason—you are in business.

Once you believe that your customers are number one, you have to figure out what that means to them. For most it means that you will serve them promptly and fix their problems. But it means more than that. It means you will invest time and resources, you'll put yourself out, and you'll focus all your energy on helping them, rather than spending time and resources on yourself.

Emerson's passage quoted earlier implies that ideally when you contribute to someone else's success, you will succeed yourself. When lunch must be catered, our training center often uses a nearby small restaurant. It's a small business with great customer service, and we like to patronize local companies like that. When we occasionally drop in for breakfast, our money is "no good" there according to Bobby, the owner. We don't expect it, but it's nice.

Your belief system goes hand-in-hand with your behavior. In fact, your beliefs will follow your behavior. Try up-serving every customer you have, and observe the results. Take every encounter one step further. You have to up-serve first, but you will find your own success growing right alongside that of your customers.

How you up-serve is important as well. The techniques that you use in up-serving—careful questioning, great listening skills, up-front contracts, bonding and rapport skills, going the extra mile—all of these techniques come under the "how" banner.

Success in customer service can be compared to a three-legged stool. The first leg is attitude—your beliefs around how customers are valued and treated. The second leg is technique—the ability of your people to question, sell, listen, communicate, inform and build relationships. The third leg is behavior—the consistent use of, and accountability to, the techniques that result in customer loyalty and increased sales. If one of these three is missing, the stool (delivery of great customer service) falls down. Bending over backwards means doing whatever is necessary to ensure the customer is served. Completely. To his complete satisfaction. Every time.

Treating long-term customers like it is the first time you've worked with them will keep the relationship fresh and ward off encroachments by the competition.

44. DO MORE THAN YOU'RE PAID FOR

Again, Emerson's passage quoted earlier describes a customer-care model that elevates service to a best-in-class model. When customer-service providers have a belief system that positively influences their behaviors around customers and coworkers, the natural outcome is up-service.

What does up-service look like? Over the years while training customer-service providers, I've heard hundreds of stories of "over and above." I prefer to think of these examples as human kindness paid forward.

> Our local power company was stretched thin after a huge winter ice storm that knocked out dozens of city blocks during the holidays. Angry customers were complaining they were having to cancel dinner parties or move in with relatives. One elderly gentleman called several times asking when he could expect his power to be restored. When asked why it was so important to him, he explained that he

was the caregiver for his wife with Alzheimer's. He worried that if he moved her out of their cold home, it would be such a setback for her, she may not be able to come home again. Within 15 minutes, a crew was pulled from other locations around the city and his power was restored.

What does it mean to do more than you are paid for? It means that you might stay after work when there's a job to finish when you only get paid until 5:00; it means making a special trip to drive a late order to a customer when you could have told him he'd have it tomorrow; it means making three extra calls trying to find a special product for a customer when you could have said, "Try XZY Company." It means constantly being aware of opportunities to add value, help out, make things easier and be of service to another person, without the thought of remuneration or recognition.

This is the "wow" service that people remark on to their friends and family. This is the up-serving that a customer knows you didn't have to do, but you went over and above to perform.

The surest way to damage a relationship is not with criticism; it is with indifference. When it looks like you don't care about a customer relationship—whether it's due to dirty shop windows, poor telephone etiquette or a late shipment without notice—you drive a wedge between you and your customer. It takes years to create a good customer relationship and sometimes only seconds to destroy it.

Behavior that is over and above, that your competition

wouldn't contemplate, is the behavior that builds relationships, loyalty and word of mouth. A genuine desire to help and an attitude that exudes care is the basis of this behavior. Only a workforce that is truly engaged will practice this kind of customer experience.

Emerson's philosophy says that when you give first, it will come back to you in time. That giving has to be done freely and without expectation. Up-serving means that when you do more than you're paid for, eventually you'll be rewarded for more than you do.

45. FIX PROBLEMS BEFORE THEY HAPPEN

Most companies have become very good at reducing their reaction time to customer problems. But what if you could stop problems before they happen? What if you took a proactive approach to customer service? What would that mean for the company? What would it mean for customers?

A large retail bank recently instituted a reward system for frontline staff. It wasn't a spiff on increased numbers or a commission on new business. Rather, it was a reward system for finding problems before they happened. Frontline staff was challenged to recognize and solve customer issues in a way that would benefit customers and help them avoid future problems. One staff member discovered that federal tax laws would require customers to pay tax on benefits unless they were transferred to a different kind of account. Once he began to mention that to customers, they were thrilled to have that information. There was no particular benefit to the bank apart from the huge amount of goodwill it generated among customers. The employee received a reward.

From technology sectors to retail-to-retail, proactively anticipating problems with every change and steering customers in the right direction will avoid damaged relationships in the future. For employees, it may involve a mind shift. Up-serving means thinking ahead and anticipating every pitfall, problem, roadblock or challenge your customer might encounter while buying or using your product.

This means looking at customers not as consumers of your product or service, but as people with challenges that your product knowledge can help. It means thinking ahead and imagining every issue that might arise. It means gaining an understanding of the customers' applications and circumstances by asking penetrating questions that give the whole picture. Only then can you foresee any problems and make a plan to avoid or eliminate those problems.

Perhaps it's a training need, or a modification is required. It may be an adjustment to a contract that gives better protection, or it may be bundling services to lower prices. Whatever it is, the message to the customer will be that you have his best interests at heart, not a concern over your next sale. Up-serving customers means anticipating problems and proactively fixing them before they're problems.

46. ALLOW CUSTOMERS TO RING THE BELL

Visiting a customer's busy auto parts counter recently, I noticed a large ship bell mounted near the door with a long rope attached and a sign that said: "Ring the bell if you've received great service today!"

As a gentleman left, he gave the rope a good pull. The clear bell rang loudly, to which the entire staff yelled: "Thank you!"

That bell gave customers an instant, fun way to provide feedback on their experience. It also gave staff a goal and a positive result from good customer service. Like Pavlov's dogs, they longed to hear that bell.

Too often people either don't ask for immediate feedback on service or they ask customers to go online and fill out a survey as they pay for their items. In these cases, feedback may more often be negative. It is rare that staff receive positive feedback on their customer service. Feedback that is easy or fun to give is more likely to be forthcoming. Here are a few guidelines: asking questions is the best way to focus attention on the kind of information you are seeking; keep it short—five questions are the limit; include the "one" question—"If there were one thing we could have done better/differently today to improve your experience, what would that be?"; and finally, have a reward for the feedback.

Get creative around receiving feedback and then ensure the feedback gets back to the people who need it—your frontline staff. One company I know plasters the walls of their lunchroom with customer feedback forms for all to read. The good ones are circled in bright green markers, and the ones of opportunities for improvement or lessons learned are in bright yellow. However you choose to gather feedback, make sure that valuable information doesn't end up filed in a drawer. If it does, why did you ask?

Up-serving requires the use of feedback in a constant improvement loop that involves staff at all levels. You'll prove to your staff and customers that you are serious about customer up-service.

47. KEEP IN TOUCH TO KEEP RELATIONSHIPS

As John's phone rang, he glanced at the caller ID and noted it was ABC Paper Products calling.

What do they want this time? he thought. *They only call when they want to sell me the latest special.*

It was true. ABC Paper had aggressive salespeople who called often, but every call was always the same: "What do you need to buy today? We've got a great deal on..."

But often when John called them for paper, all he got was a busy signal. He was tired of it.

Keeping in touch with customers on a consistent basis should be more than sales calls. Although most customers want a purely professional relationship, they also want to know they are more than just the sum of their year's purchases to a vendor. They want to feel appreciated.

Arranging to have a number of touch points with a customer over the year is a planning and execution exercise. Even though the sending of emails is government-regulated these days (so be sure to get your customers' approval before sending), a brief newsletter or industry information post that has value to your customer is a good basis for regular touch points by email. Perhaps it is a "tip of the week" or updates on industry changes or new product updates. These should not necessarily be sales-oriented, but they should have value to the customer.

Also by email, a brief customer-service survey gives customers the opportunity to give honest feedback on their experience with your company. People who wouldn't take time to write a letter of complaint or compliment will click through a survey and give you valuable feedback on your service levels and people. It's also a touch point for contact with those customers and tells them their opinion is important to you, as well as their patronage.

Handwritten notes after a particularly large sale or a difficult negotiation are often appreciated. Anyone can dash off a quick email and forget it, but a handwritten card shows you took the time and cared. Handwritten notes can also be effective with customers who haven't purchased in a while.

A telephone call is the most powerful tool you have for touching customers. Some customer-care departments will provide the president or CEO of the company with a list of customers weekly to call to thank for their business. These calls may result in more business, but they are not meant to be a solicitation; they are simply a "thank you" for doing business and a show of appreciation for customer loyalty. Up-serving means letting customers know you appreciate their business on a consistent basis in a variety of ways.

48. ENGAGE CUSTOMERS ON AN EMOTIONAL LEVEL

A few years ago I dropped into a small boutique with only one employee working. She was busy creating a display. She immediately approached me and asked if I could help her with something. She wanted my opinion of her display.

If she hadn't asked me over, would it have caught my eye? Would it be too much if she added these two items? She wasn't over the top or solicitous, and she engaged me instantly. She read that I was simply browsing and rather than say, "Can I help you?" she engaged me.

We continued to have a great conversation about her shop, her displays, my day and my ideas. I have since told many people what a lovely shop she has and sent her customers. What was different? She engaged me emotionally.

"Can I help you?" is a business question. "Can I get your help on this?" taps into a person's emotions.

Engaging customers on an emotional level is reflective of the levels of conversation you have with others. There is the sur-

Sandler Rules for Up-Serving

face level—clichés that you would share with a stranger in an elevator—"Nice day, huh?" The next level down is information sharing—"Let me tell you about our specials today"; "Looks like rain." The third level is the emotional level, and it requires asking someone about his thoughts and feelings. In the story above, being asked to share my thoughts about the employee's display immediately put me on a more intimate relationship footing.

Depending on the business, it may be more challenging to get to the emotional level. In a clothing store, rather than saying the traditional, "Oh, that looks so nice on you," you could choose to ask, "How do you feel in this one?" Tapping into people's emotions is the surest way to do two things: build a relationship based on trust, and access their decision-making level. People make purchasing decisions emotionally. They justify them intellectually.

Even if someone is purchasing widgets, rather than say, "Need anything else today?" you might try, "Having problems with your usual widgets?" It's more likely to give you an emotional response. People seldom tell others about a customer-service experience that was merely satisfactory. Happy experiences, they will remember—and repeat to others. "Happy" means there was an emotional connection with another person.

Up-serving means tapping into a deeper level of emotion and ensuring your customers are happy (an emotional word) rather than simply satisfied (an intellectual state).

EPILOGUE

How do you create a customer-focused, revenue-producing, up-serving, high-performing, service-delivering organization that results in loyal, happy customers? There is no magic dust, no special greeting nor secret handshake that will produce these results. There are many things you need to do right. It all starts with a belief—the belief that the growth of your company, in fact its very existence, depends on your customers. Customers deserve more than they pay for; they deserve respect, patience, kindness, your time and your help.

The rules describe the guidelines for investing in customer care, starting with hiring the right people. Often people are hired too quickly; there is a hole in the organization and management wants to fill it quickly. They don't take the time to understand the job requirements, match those to the right assessments, write the right job listing to attract the right candidates or screen candidates properly to qualify against described job competencies. When you start with the wrong people, it's hard to keep your business on track.

Often people neglect to set expectations of the highest standards of customer service, sales, relationship building and communications through ongoing training. They can find themselves disappointed with staff behavior when expectations haven't been communicated or modeled effectively. Where does the responsibility fall? The role of frontline service providers can be described as "professional communicator," yet they haven't been supported with soft skills and communication training.

Neither are they given support in sales skills, yet they are often expected to fulfill that role. They haven't been given a process to make selling more comfortable. They are, however, blamed when the results aren't there. Often they are replaced with more employees who are hired quickly and aren't trained. The insanity is, of course, that companies continue to repeat this, getting the same results.

Everyone needs support and reminders about communication skills and the process for effective selling. In fact, they need a smooth process for almost every function for which they have responsibility. Yet they need the freedom to make decisions and sometimes even mistakes. They need to understand the essentials of up-service. What does it mean, and how do you achieve it?

CHANGING TIMES

The rules for customer service have changed with advances in technology. There are new rules around communication and the effects of a negative customer experience can have on your business. One negative review can be posted on the Internet and read by hundreds or thousands within hours.

You don't own your customers. They are free to make different choices at any time. It may only take one bad experience to send them to your competition, who will welcome them with open arms.

It's not the big gestures or the over-the-top deliveries that count, although they may make Internet chatter. It's the day-to-day, relentlessly consistent, customer-focused service that differentiates you from your competition. It's leadership in instituting that focus. It's responsiveness to customer needs, and that doesn't mean the lowest price or biggest discounts.

If you are thinking that these 48 Rules are common sense, you are absolutely correct. You may believe that they're simple and intuitive, and that's right, too. The question is, how many of these do you actually implement? Do you know what your frontline people are saying and doing daily? Are they reactive rather than proactive? How busy are they, versus being productive?

Everyone has room for improvement. Everyone can reach higher, be more productive, do better, perform more consistently and have better results. The secret is to create a plan, get everyone on board, hire to it, train to it, implement it and hold people accountable for it every day. Simple. But it takes a huge commitment from all levels to make it happen. Without that commitment, nothing will change. A commitment is followed by a decision, and a decision is followed by behavior. Behavior, behavior, behavior. It's the only thing that will, or ever has, made any difference to any organization.

Experience says that buy-in for corporate cultural change must involve customer-service supervisors. Outcomes of training may be destroyed by supervisors who believe it either will not work or in some way doesn't complement their own belief system. They become part of the problem instead of part of the solution. When supervisors feel marginalized, they can become passive aggressive—saying the right things, but communicating negativity to their people. In this situation, customer-service providers are caught in a no-win and unfair position. Spending time involving the supervisor in creating positive change gives the best return on investment.

THE FUTURE OF CUSTOMER EXPERIENCE

A large airline was recently asked (off the record) about their customer-service department going forward. They replied that they "won't have one." They will be replacing all their staff with automation. Within a few years, all customer service will be done online, with no live interaction at all.

Epilogue

Is this the future of customer care? There is no doubt that automation and computerization can do it cheaper and faster. But can anything besides people read customers' body language, respond to their tonality and recognize subtle buying signals? Will live customer-care providers be the differentiator that grows your business in the future?

Technology has infiltrated customer service, mainly in the tracking and measurement of customer experience. There are programs to track what people are saying about you on social media—tracking user-generated content to evaluate sentiment and attempt to engage people. If a customer has a bad experience, companies want to track and find out about it. But measuring whether the customer is a brand advocate or detractor through things like the Net Promoter Score is an after-the-fact exercise.

The question is, does this technology give the customer a better experience with the company? If it helps customers save time, they want it. If it is too complicated to be a time saver, it will frustrate them. If there's no live help, they will wander away to "find a person to help." Will customer service end up being a face on a screen?

Picking up a rental car at the airport recently, Betty noticed people patiently standing in line to talk to a customer-service representative while a computerized stand stood empty. She boldly stepped forward and entered her reservation number, and a friendly face appeared on the screen and easily walked her through the process in less than four minutes. In another two minutes she was in her rental car and leaving.

The woman on the screen was sitting in her home office hundreds of miles away, not using expensive transportation and time to get to and from work, not needing to stand on her feet for hours at a time and being there to make lunch for her kids. For Betty, that was a live interaction with a person and a good technology-based experience.

Today you can go to a movie without interacting with another person. You can plan a trip through four countries without so much as a phone call. But, if something goes wrong at the theater or on the trip, you may prefer to speak to a real person and get it solved.

It is already true that you can access customer service on a mobile device, through email and websites, through texts and face-to-face. Leading companies make all these experiences part of a cohesive customer experience with their organization. Laggard companies struggle to present a cohesive message in these forums.

Technology is already available to replace a car-rental salesperson with an avatar, but is everyone ready for that? The human tendency is engrained to want to whine, vent, complain, praise, plead, cajole, thank and vex other people. Can you do that to the same satisfaction with an avatar? I doubt any avatar could be programmed with the nuances in tonality, body language and creative problem solving needed to deal with human beings day in and day out. (I may eventually be proved wrong about that.)

How it is delivered will certainly evolve, but the basics of customer service will remain the same: communication, nurturing and connecting people to products and services that fit their needs. To the degree that automation improves and supports a great customer experience, it's wonderful. Yet humans will always need the human touch, and the 48 Rules I've shared with you will help to provide the person-to-person interaction that is an indispensable requirement of great service.

Look for these other books
on shop.sandler.com:

Prospect the Sandler Way

Transforming Leaders the Sandler Way

Selling Professional Services the Sandler Way

Accountability the Sandler Way

Selling Technology the Sandler Way

LinkedIn the Sandler Way

CONGRATULATIONS!

Customer Service the Sandler Way
includes a complimentary seminar!

Take this opportunity to personally experience the non-traditional sales training and reinforcement coaching that has been recognized internationally for decades.

Companies in the Fortune 1000 as well as thousands of small- to medium-sized businesses choose Sandler for sales, leadership, management, and a wealth of other skill-building programs. Now, it's your turn, and it's free!

You'll learn the latest practical, tactical, feet-in-the-street sales methods directly from your neighborhood Sandler trainers! They're knowledgeable, friendly and informed about your local selling environment.

Here's how you redeem YOUR FREE SEMINAR invitation.

1. Go to www.Sandler.com and click on Find Training Location (top blue bar).
2. Select your location.
3. Review the list of all the Sandler trainers in your area.
4. Call your local Sandler trainer, mention *Customer Service the Sandler Way* and reserve your place at the next seminar!